Capitol Hill Library

NO LONGER PROPERTY OF
SEATTLE PUBLIC LIBRARY

JAN 14 2019

"This is the most insightful book I've read about parenting adopted teens. Naftzger draws from her own experience as an adoptee and a therapist to offer parents practical tools for improving communication with their child, without ever being preachy or prescriptive. Most importantly, she honors the emotions, integrity and intellectual capacity of the adopted teen at every turn, helping parents better understand the complexity of their child's experience."

—*Nicole Opper, Director/Producer,* Off and Running: An American Coming of Age Story

"After my adoptive daughter's teen years, I appreciate even more the value of Katie Naftzger's keen insights and sage advice. By sharing adoptees' stories and empathizing, as only a once teen adoptee can, Naftzger ably steers adoptive parents through the choppy waters of adolescence."

—*Melissa Ludtke, author of* Touching Home in China: In Search of Missing Girlhoods

"I loved *Parenting in the Eye of the Storm.* While Katie Naftzger defines her work as 'The Adoptive Parent's Guide to Navigating the Teen Years,' I found it to be so very much more. Inside this book I found priceless wisdom and insight into the wounded hearts of adopted teens. The tools Ms Naftzger shares here are like a flashlight and compass for parents to light the way for their struggling adopted teen and bring them home. Well worth the investment of time!"

—*Nancy Thomas, author of* When Love is Not Enough: A Guide to Parenting Children with Reactive Attachment Disorder

"Naftzger provides useful day-to-day insights and practical suggestions for adoptive families with teens. Her book is filled with personal accounts and situations that are both from her personal experience as well as her clinical practice. This combination of lived and professional insight in the adoption world is rare and makes this book a must-have for all adoptive families."

—*Iris Chin Ponte Ph.D., President of Ponte and Chau Consulting Inc. and Director of the Henry Frost Children's Program*

D0011628

of related interest

Adoption at the Movies
A Year of Adoption Friendly Movie Nights to Get Your Family Talking
Addison Cooper
ISBN 978 1 78592 709 6
eISBN 978 1 78450 275 1

Parenting Adopted Teenagers
Advice for the Adolescent Years
Rachel Staff
ISBN 978 1 84905 604 5
eISBN 978 1 78450 069 6

Attaching in Adoption
Practical Tools for Today's Parents
Deborah D. Gray
ISBN 978 1 84905 890 2
eISBN 978 0 85700 606 6

Can I tell you about Adoption?
A Guide for Friends, Family and Professionals
Anne Braff Brodzinsky
ISBN 978 1 84905 942 8
eISBN 978 0 85700 759 9
Can I tell you about...? series

The Unofficial Guide to Adoptive Parenting
The Small Stuff, the Big Stuff and the Stuff in Between
Sally Donovan
ISBN 978 1 84905 536 9
eISBN 978 0 85700 959 3

Why Can't My Child Behave?
Empathic Parenting Strategies that Work for Adoptive and Foster Families
Dr Amber Elliott
ISBN 978 1 84905 339 6
eISBN 978 0 85700 671 4

PARENTING
IN THE EYE OF THE
STRM

The Adoptive Parent's
Guide to Navigating
the Teen Years

Katie Naftzger

Foreword by Adam Pertman

Jessica Kingsley *Publishers*
London and Philadelphia

First published in 2017
by Jessica Kingsley Publishers
73 Collier Street
London N1 9BE, UK
and
400 Market Street, Suite 400
Philadelphia, PA 19106, USA

www.jkp.com

Copyright © Katie Naftzger 2017
Foreword copyright © Adam Pertman 2017

Front cover image source: Shutterstock®.

All rights reserved. No part of this publication may be reproduced in any
material form (including photocopying, storing in any medium by electronic
means or transmitting) without the written permission of the copyright owner
except in accordance with the provisions of the law or under terms of a licence
issued in the UK by the Copyright Licensing Agency Ltd. www.cla.co.uk or in
overseas territories by the relevant reproduction rights organisation, for details
see www.ifrro.org. Applications for the copyright owner's written permission to
reproduce any part of this publication should be addressed to the publisher.

Warning: The doing of an unauthorised act in relation to a copyright work
may result in both a civil claim for damages and criminal prosecution.

Library of Congress Cataloging in Publication Data
A CIP catalog record for this book is available from the Library of Congress

British Library Cataloguing in Publication Data
A CIP catalogue record for this book is available from the British Library

ISBN 978 1 78592 701 0
eISBN 978 1 78450 244 7

Printed and bound in the United States

Contents

Foreword

A few years ago, I was talking on the phone with a colleague about some work we were planning to do together. Toward the end of the call, when the subject turned to our families, she asked how old my two children were. "They're both teenagers," I said. Without skipping a beat, she replied, "Oh, I'm sorry."

Yes, it was a joke and we both laughed. It obviously was funny, however, largely because it was rooted in reality; that is, for a broad array of reasons related to normative human development, raising an adolescent—almost any adolescent—can be challenging. Add greater, ongoing complexity to the picture, such as divorce or single-parenting or adoption (among many others), and the job invariably gets more complicated, more stressful and more difficult.

That's why there are therapists, support groups and parenting books, right? Because one thing all moms and dads learn every day is that love alone is not enough to raise a child. We also need experience, knowledge and resources. Alas, one of the many results of the secrecy and stigma that has enveloped adoption for generations is that adoptive parents too often do not receive the knowledge and tools that would benefit them and, consequently, their sons and daughters.

All of which is why this book, *Parenting in the Eye of the Storm: The Adoptive Parent's Guide to Navigating the Teen Years*, is so important. Every stage of adopted children's lives is obviously significant, and understanding the sometimes-challenging issues of every stage enables parents to provide better nurture and guidance. But there is a dearth of well-researched, thoughtfully presented books on the specific subject of parenting children and youth during the period of their lives that is already so complicated, so fraught with issues relating to identity, independence and family connections.

In *Parenting in the Eye of the Storm*, Katie Naftzger takes adoptive parents through the teen years with a wisdom born of her extensive research, her years as a therapist for adopted teens and their families, and her own lived experience as a person who was adopted (from Korea). It's a powerful combination, and the result is that she is able to provide insights and suggestions that are not only well-informed, but also are very useful in a practical, day-to-day way.

At the same time, the author recognizes that adoptive parents don't just need information and insights. They also need answers, guidance and understanding—and a roadmap for fitting all the pieces together. The most valuable thing about this book is that it provides that roadmap.

For example, in her first chapter, "Layers of Loss for Adoptees," Katie delves into the emotional experiences of adopted teens with common losses such as of safety, as well as less-examined ones such as loss of accountability and of innocence. Then she takes the reader through four parenting tasks: un-rescuing, setting adoption-sensitive limits, having connecting conversations and envisioning their adopted teens' future, in that order. From there, she delves into the vital topics of race and mental health, and concludes by discussing why self-care is so important for adoptive parents, not just for their wellbeing but also to model for their teens.

At the bottom line, this must-read book for adoptive parents is an invaluable addition to a toolbox that, until now, had too many missing pieces. My only complaint about

Parenting in the Eye of the Storm is this: Why wasn't it around when my wife and I needed it? No joke.

Adam Pertman
President, CEO and Founder of the National Center on
Adoption and Permanency

Acknowledgments

To Lisa Tener, Calla Devlin and Lynne Griffith, thank you for your insight and feedback.

Thank you to Rose Kent and Martha Crawford for believing in me. And, to the late Betty Jean Lifton who told me, "If you want to write a book, write the book."

Thanks to my friends who were with me all the way. Thank you to my mother-in-law, my best cheerleader. And, thank you to my adoptive parents who have stayed true to their values of serving the underserved and unacknowledged. Lastly, thank you to my wonderful family for giving me the time and support that I needed to finish.

Introduction

Jennifer was an adoptive parent who contacted me requesting a parent consultation regarding her 15-year-old daughter adopted from China, Maddie.

"As I mentioned on the phone, I saw you speak at an adoption conference four or five years ago. I think you were talking about the adoption groups you were doing at the time. Anyway, for me, the fact that you're an adoptee is huge. I mean, I'm her mom and I love her but I'm not adopted and don't know what that feels like."

Jennifer's voice quivered just slightly and she looked away.

"A few weeks ago Maddie told me that she's been unhappy. She said that she's lonely. And she's been crying a lot, almost every day. I told her that we could go to China and maybe even search for her birth parents but that didn't seem to help. She just told me that I don't get it and that I'll never understand what she's going through. But then she said something about how maybe life wasn't worth it. It scared me. That's when I dug out your card and called you."

"Has she ever been like this before?"

"No, not at all. I don't know what happened. Maddie was wonderful. She was so happy, never cried. Her teachers adored her."

I asked:

"So, she didn't get angry much when she was a kid?"

"No."

Jennifer thought for a second.

"Oh, she got mad at me a few times when she was younger. Twice, she said, 'I hate you. You're not my real mom anyway.' But later on she apologized. I think she felt really bad about it."

Jennifer rubbed her forehead as she teared up.

"It just breaks my heart out to see her like this."

Sitting across from me, Jennifer flopped back on the couch.

Jennifer went on to explain that she previously talked with her individual therapist about her difficulties with Maddie. Her therapist believed that Maddie was testing Jennifer's resolve as a parent and suggested that Jennifer keep reassuring Maddie that she loves her, and will never abandon her. Her therapist also suggested that Jennifer write her a letter reiterating that message.

But when Jennifer did that it seemed to make things worse.

"She got really angry with me when I gave her the letter, almost like I had somehow hurt her even more. I have no idea why. Now, she barely acknowledges me. I don't know what to think, whether this is an adoption thing, or what's going on."

Jennifer sighed again, frustrated.

Many therapists working with adoptive parents would have probably recommended a variation of that of Jennifer's therapist—"I'll be there for you, I love you and I'll never abandon you." She was right in that it may well have been a test, but a different one. Maddie's internal question was not "Will you leave me?" but "Can you tolerate my emotional anguish which is a part of me?"

But adopted teens don't want or need reassurance. They want to feel less alone and more understood. That requires an entirely different message—"I understand what you're saying, it's not easy, these things take time, maybe even a lifetime. It's really hard."

MY BACKGROUND

My adoption experience is broad and deep. I am Korean-born, internationally and transracially adopted. My life experience informs my work, and my work informs my life. My interest in helping others began long before I became a therapist. Although I can't confirm this, doing this kind of work with individuals and families was in my blood, as the saying goes.

My adoptive parents were loving, kind and compassionate. But they didn't know what my younger sister, also Korean and adopted, and I needed, especially during the teen years. My parents learned the hard way that love is not enough. They would be the first to tell you that, if they could go back, they would have parented us differently.

My first life lesson—it won't get any easier.

This is the book they needed.

Although I had already been doing clinical work for a few years my focus on adoption really began in 2002, when I co-led a Chinese adopted girls group, the first of many. This was one of the first groups of its kind after the one-child policy took effect in 1980. In a group where Asian adoptees were in the majority, we were able to explore ideas and feelings in ways that weren't usually possible in everyday life.

It's more difficult to feel empowered alone.

Feeling abandoned and being abandoned are two different things. Being abandoned is a tragedy but feeling abandoned is a part of growing up. When you avoid that feeling at all costs, it makes the already daunting task of growing up even more difficult for your adopted teen. For instance, Jennifer realized that she had been rescuing Maddie from stressful situations, limiting her chance to develop valuable coping skills. Also, Jennifer didn't want her daughter to feel abandoned, a feeling that many adoptive parents share. For example, if Maddie had a difficult day at school, her mother picked her up early, no questions asked.

Until then, Jennifer's skill set had been more focused on comfort and warmth. She was involved, loving, attentive and reassuring. Jennifer needed to cultivate four skill sets that address the unique needs of your adopted teen.

These are:

1. "unrescuing" your adopted teen

2. setting adoption-sensitive limits

3. having connected conversations

4. helping your teen envision their future.

We worked on setting "adoption-sensitive" limits. Turns out that Jennifer hadn't been doing as much of that as she should have.

She said: "I'm not much of a disciplinarian, I guess. I just want her to be happy all the time. I thought that if I could just get through to her, things would be better."

Actually, Jennifer had it backwards. In order to strengthen their relationship, Maddie needed to see that Jennifer could stand up to her. Maddie needed to see that Jennifer could say no, even if it meant being the bad guy.

We also worked on setting "adoption-sensitive" limits that encouraged Maddie to take more responsibility for her own feelings and decisions. Jennifer also learned about how to have the connecting conversation. This is a conversation after which the adopted teen feels more understood, less alone and more connected with their parent. And, finally, I helped Jennifer to understand how difficult it was for Maddie to see herself as someone with a future. Keith, a 17-year-old adopted from Russia, said, during our interview for this book,

"Yeah, it's hard to know where you're going if you don't know where you've been."

Years ago, I suggested to a father, whose nine-year-old son I was working with, that we have a family meeting. The father asked why, then smiled, saying, "You want the truth!"

I do want the truth. The family unit is a powerful force in the lives of adopted teens. Along with the specific issues of the adopted teen, I'm interested in learning about the culture of the family—communication, conflict and relationships.

In addition to the four tasks for adoptive parents, I discuss two special topics in detail – race and mental health. In the chapter on race (Chapter 7) I discuss the challenges of being born into one race and raised into another. In examples from work and life I discuss a different take on white privilege, norms versus stereotypes and differences between the Black experience and the Asian experience. I also explore another way to talk about racism and what parents can do to support this process of racial identity. Although I use the example of Asian adoptees, my hope is that it will be helpful even if you're outside of that demographic.

Research suggests that adopted teens are more likely to be diagnosed with Attention Deficit Hyperactivity Disorder (ADHD) and Oppositional Defiant Disorder. In addition, they are more at risk for making a suicide attempt. In the chapter on mental health (Chapter 8) I discuss suicidality as a survival issue, and possible ways to understand why adoptees are at higher risk. You also learn how to seek help if and when you need it, and how working through the four tasks is a proactive way to prevent further tragedies. Lastly, I discuss the importance of self-care for adoptive parents.

HOW TO USE THIS BOOK

Know that this book is best read from the beginning, not as a reference. Each section is carefully chosen to follow the one before. You'll undermine your progress if you skip ahead. I generally refer to teens as being from ages 12 to 19 or grades 7–12. I generally refer to teens that were adopted when they were younger. I offer examples from life and work with altered names and other specifics for purposes of confidentiality. The insights and strategies you learn are based on my over 15 years of experience working with adopted teens, parents and families, current research and a lifetime as an adoptee.

Terms

I prefer the terms teen and teenhood as opposed to adolescence because I like to mirror the language of families. Most families don't say, "Is this adolescent behavior," so I also don't. I will also use the term white and Caucasian interchangeably. I will use the term adoptee although I know that many take issue with that term. To me, it's accurate shorthand. Especially as we're into teenhood, I feel that the word attachment has more of a clinical/research connotation than it does a place in our heartfelt, personal conversation about families. Many clinicians and parents include reactive attachment disorder in their repertoire. I respect that but feel that for me in my work and life talking about relationships and emotional connectedness feels more authentic. I will use the term birth family and biological family. Often I will use birth family in relation to international adoptions and biological family in relation to domestic adoptions.

Bottom line

These years make or break families. There's so much hidden potential in the teen years. This book is unique in that it's not about what your adopted teen can do differently; it's about how to *parent* them differently. Understanding your adopted teen better is just the beginning. You learn how to *use* that knowledge to change the way that you parent. With your love and commitment and my personal and professional expertise we'll reach two important goals—to help to prepare them for adulthood and to stay connected for the long haul. If you do the work, the learning of insights and strategies will serve you well. It will be worthwhile. I want each family to live up to their potential.

Whether you're struggling or coasting there's more to learn. Let's get started!

Chapter 1

Layers of Loss for Adoptees

LOSS OF CONTINUITY

Imagine walking into a movie 20 minutes late. Everyone else is already there, settled in. And, as you watch, you're trying to figure out what you missed. Did that character come up earlier? Were they always in the city? You weren't privy to the beginning of the movie, so you missed that first scene, how the cast of characters was introduced and the tenor of the movie in general. Was there something shocking in the opening of the movie which was watched by everyone except you, and which subsequently makes the movie make sense in some kind of "big picture" way? Throughout the movie, you're asking yourself, do other people know something that I don't?

You try to tell yourself to just forget about it. After all, you're there, right? Dwelling on the part you missed is just ruining what you're watching right now. After all, you've seen most of it. You try to put it behind you, but you can't. Everyone else in the theater seems to be having a ball. So, you try to join in, be a part of the group, as if you were just like everyone else. You smile and laugh like they do, and maybe you even forget for a moment that you had missed anything.

Then you overhear someone referring to the beginning of the movie, "Oh, so that's why she was in a hospital bed before." Hospital bed, what? Now, you're even more confused and disoriented.

Your friend says cheerily, "Don't worry. You didn't miss much!"

How would that be for you? What if you couldn't watch it again and there was no one else to ask? Does the lack of continuity frustrate you or haunt you? Would you feel angry, helpless? Or, perhaps you feel sorry for yourself. You might ask yourself, why me? Perhaps you promise yourself never to be late again, or do anything else to jeopardize your wellbeing, for that matter.

You don't even try to tell people what you're going through anymore because it just seems to create tension in your relationships. They just keep telling you how great you are, and eventually you agree because that's what they seem to need from you. They didn't get it, and you end up feeling even worse. You thought they understood but maybe they don't. Now, you feel lost, angry and alone.

This is the first of eight losses embedded in the adoption story—loss of *continuity*.

Your adopted teen's story is their own and unique in its meaning. Some were born domestically, others internationally. Some began in an orphanage or residential care, others in foster or kinship care. Some were relinquished at birth, others after multiple traumas and countless placements. Some have open adoptions with ongoing contact with their biological parents while others don't. The adoption community is rich in its diversity and depth. They connect through overarching themes of loss and vulnerability.

There are eight layers of loss embedded in the adoption story. Those losses are:

1. loss of continuity

2. loss of safety

3. loss of control

4. loss of closure

5. loss of trust in adults

6. loss of innocence

7. loss of worth

8. loss of accountability

The story

I was in graduate school studying social work, in a class on the use of narratives or stories in clinical work with families. In class, we were asked to share a story from our life that defined us in some way. One student talked about losing her finger when she battled cancer; another talked about his bitter divorce. Everyone seemed to have that defining story at the ready, except for me. My mind was a complete blank. All I needed was one. Why, then, was it so hard for me?

Just then, I realized. I needed to tell the story I never knew, my life before I was adopted. I was born somewhere in Korea, in an unknown setting, from someone whose identity is unknown. There was also an unknown father whose location was unknown. Somehow, towards the beginning, I ended up in an adoption agency. I couldn't find the words to tell it, because I didn't *have* the story. There was no one to ask. And, apart from a sparse adoption file, no information.

I had no words, no witnesses and no documentation. In that moment, I couldn't move forward without it.

Being adopted is not just an isolated event. It's a part of one's identity that is constantly evolving and changing.

LOSS OF SAFETY

It was in my first meeting with Nora, 13, adopted from Korea at five months old. She had been crying a lot for the past week talking about how much she missed her birth mother. That's when her mom got in touch with me.

In those first few meetings, I learned a lot about Nora. She was close with her adoptive parents who were responsive and thoughtful. She had lots of friends and was doing well in school. But there was an aspect of her story that still haunted her. Based on the sparse information in her file, Nora believed that she was left outside of a social welfare agency, and later found and brought in by a worker.

"I could have died," she said.

Her eyes flooded with tears and she said it again.

"I could have died."

Those words had never seen the light of day. It was like a confession. Although she didn't have the facts, what could have happened frightened her. Like other survivors she had come too close to not making it through. She knew that she had been at risk. She had spoken with her adoptive mother about most things but not this.

What did she need from me? A witness. There are often no witnesses in the lives of adoptees. Although I wasn't there, I could be a witness for her story. She didn't need me to tell her that she was safe or loved. She didn't need me to explain why that might have happened to her. If I had responded that way, she might have sensed that I wanted her to feel better and tried to oblige. Then, she would be doing it for me not for her.

Calm and heartfelt, I said, "That must have been so scary for you to be all alone like that. You were afraid that something would happen to you," to which she responded tearily, "I know."

In time, she didn't need to talk about it anymore. For now, it was as if a burden had been lifted.

After four months, in my final parent meeting her father said, "Wow, it seems there was a lot of progress in a short amount of time."

Yes, the power of witnessing cannot be underestimated.

Adopted teens survived something that was beyond their control. An infant or young child without parents who love and care for them is at risk. Although they may not remember what they went through, they are well aware that their physical and emotional safety was compromised. Life fell apart for a while. Often, there was trauma, relinquishment, abuse and instability. The adoption story is not just of abandonment or relinquishment. The adoption story is about survival. Some survived the relinquishment and then were safe in a stable adoptive home. Others had to survive again and again.

LOSS OF CONTROL

Tasha, 15 years old, lived with her aunt after being physically and emotionally abused by her biological mother. She was pulled out of the home when she was 11. One of her friend's mothers contacted social services after she saw the gashes on Tasha's legs. As a freshman in high school she had a physical altercation with a female peer after she accused Tasha of sleeping with the peer's boyfriend, which Tasha denied. Tasha had already been diagnosed with depression a few years back, but then she began experiencing feelings that directly related to her previous trauma. Tasha said that she felt numb and detached much of the time. She struggled to do what she knew was right, like practicing safe sex and advocating for herself in relationships. Her memories were tangled up in her mind. Sometimes all she could see were images that she wished she could forget.

She sat across from me, tall, medium build, mixed race of African-American and Caucasian. Her jeans and short-sleeved shirt were just a size too tight, staying in trend with her peers. Her brown shoulder-length hair had been straightened, no makeup.

We talked about her history of abuse and trauma, what had happened and in what ways it continues to haunt her.

Then, Tasha said, "I don't know how I survived. I was lucky." She swallowed a lump in her throat when she said it, but they weren't tears of relief. She was lucky, but not happy. In her darker moments, Tasha wished that she hadn't been so lucky.

The theme of luck in the adoption story is tinged with loss. Nora was lucky that she survived the relinquishment. Tasha was lucky that she survived those years of abuse. Inherent in being one of the lucky ones in adoption is the second chance at a family and a life, a chance that others didn't get. It implies that you survived something that others didn't. Not everyone has the same amount of luck. Being lucky also means that you were dependent on the kindness of strangers. This is a precarious place to be. Adoptees are *lucky* to have the things that most take for granted. One shouldn't have to be lucky to have a loving family. To be lucky is to have no control whatsoever. That is the loss.

LOSS OF CLOSURE

Over summer vacation, when my seven-year-old son and I worked on a Frog and Toad puzzle, I had to coax him to even be involved given that he preferred to just play with his Lego. But eventually he joined me and we had fun putting it together. That is until the final moment when we realized that there was that one piece missing. I tried to take it in my stride.

I said cheerily, "Oh, that happens sometimes. It was fun though!"

But inside I was more than disappointed. I was angry, and I even felt a little bit betrayed even though I had no one to blame. Should I even keep the puzzle, without that last piece? Would I ever want to put it together again? What's the point? Even though we had 99 out of 100 pieces, without that last piece, it didn't feel completely done. That feeling is a familiar one for many adopted teens, that feeling that you don't have all of the pieces that you need and there's nothing you can do about it.

When I led adoption groups and workshops, I often asked the kids what questions they would have for their birth parent if they ever met them. Often, their first question would be, "Are you alive?" That would come with many giggles, but in fact, that is our first question. The death of a loved one delineates the end of that relationship. It's not always that clear for adopted teens with their birth or biological parents. Many don't know whether their birth parents are still living. Some adoptees search for birth parents or siblings, without being able to predict the outcome. So much of the lives of adoptees is left untied.

LOSS OF TRUST IN ADULTS

Imagine that you were a young child who boarded the Titanic with your family, your parents and maybe your older sister or brother. You'd been looking forward to this for weeks. It was the trip of a lifetime. The ship was larger than life; the captain exuded confidence. The passengers were oblivious. They didn't know that there weren't enough lifeboats.

No one was prepared for everything to fall apart. And then it did.

You were the only one in your family who survived. You were one of the lucky few although you didn't feel lucky. You felt lost, scared and alone. A loving, caring family came along and agreed to take you in. They welcomed you into their home, their life. They adopted you. They loved you and you loved them. They became your new adoptive family.

You tried to put what happened out of your mind but often had nightmares replaying the sinking. You didn't tell your parents because you didn't want to upset them.

One day your adoptive parents explained to you that your father had to take a job that was far away and they were going to have to move. The only way to get there was by ship. Your parents seemed sure that everything would be fine. Is it like the Titanic you ask? They laugh. "Oh, no, sweetie, boats have come a long way since then. That was years ago!"

You were angry. You weren't there, you told them in your mind, but stayed quiet.

You decide to talk with your mom about your fears.

Your mom said, "Oh, sweetie. It'll be fine. I promise. I would never let anything happen to you."

Your mother sounds just like the captain of the Titanic did and look how that turned out. Does she not recognize the risks? Or does she recognize them but just not tell you about them? Either way, you no long trust her to tell you the truth and keep you safe.

LOSS OF INNOCENCE

Before the Boston Marathon bombing happened in 2013 I never thought anything like that could happen. It never crossed my mind. I watched it every year, loved the drama and the triumph. The kids brought the signs and the noisemakers and cheered their heads off. We live just down the street.

And then the bombing happened. My three-year-old son and I came back and were sort of resting in my bedroom. My husband came in with my daughter and said quietly, "There's been a tragedy at the marathon. The area is complete pandemonium. At least four people are dead." I didn't think my son was listening but after my husband and daughter left he said to me, "We can just go under the covers in this cave and we'll be safe there." He pulled the comforter over his head.

Everyone in our area of the city was mandated to stay inside the next day.

The police, the chase, the deaths and the heroes. It was a nightmare for the city of Boston. The city rose to the challenge but there was one thing that was really gone.

The innocence.

Even if it never happens again, it's in the books. It might not look that different. We may still be happy and enjoy the day and support the runners. Only we can tell that the innocence is missing. We don't talk about it. We just know.

For many children, there's a time when all they knew and experienced was good. They didn't have a care in the world. They didn't worry about whether they were being taken care of or whether their parents were up for the task.

Many people experience trauma in many forms. It's not just the trauma that is the loss. It's that it happened first.

LOSS OF WORTH

Becky was just eight years old, but emotionally she was younger. Becky had been adopted by her loving and dedicated foster moms, Shelby and Karen. She was referred to my therapeutic girls group because of her rages at home and extreme hyperactivity at school, along with five other girls. In one session we played a game called two truths and a lie. Each person thinks of three facts about themselves; two are true and one is the lie. The game is to guess which is the lie.

Two of the girls went before Becky. Their facts were things like how many pets they had or where they went for summer vacation.

Then it was Becky's turn. Her three facts were: I have a pet hamster, my favorite color is purple and I hate myself.

The group paused, then one of the girls said tentatively, "Was the last one the lie?"

Becky answered simply, "No, that one is true. I do hate myself. It was the second one. My favorite color is orange not purple."

"Why do you hate yourself?" I asked.

"Because I always get in trouble and get too mad in school"—her tone unchanged.

Becky wasn't asking for my pity or even my help. She just wanted us to know her better. And this was her.
I said just as simply, "Life can make it hard to feel good about yourself sometimes."

It's not uncommon for me to see adopted teens that hate aspects of their appearance. I realize that many teens are self-conscious and even unhappy about their looks, which is different than hating one's appearance.

"I just think that most of the other girls in my school are prettier than I am. I don't know why people say I'm pretty but…I'm not seeing it." Dana was a Korean-born transracial adoptee in her sophomore year of high school. Her mom Janet, Caucasian, thought that it would be helpful for Dana to have someone to talk with who looked like her. One morning, Janet overheard Dana crying as she stared at herself in the mirror.

"I just think that girls with blonde hair look a lot prettier." Dana searched my eyes trying to gauge my reaction, given that her feelings about the appearance of Asians also included me.

Instead, I asked, "What do you see when you look in the mirror, do you think?

Dana hesitated, smiled nervously. "I think I look… deformed."

"Deformed? How so?" I tried to stay neutral.

Dana said, "One eye is bigger than the other and I have that monolid." She gestured to her eyelids, making a curving motion with her finger. "I don't have that crease."

When I was young, I used to stand in front of the mirror after getting out of the shower and rub my eyes. After I would stop rubbing them there was a crease, the line that many non-Asian people have, just for a few seconds. I liked the look of it and would rub my eyes again. Somewhere along the way, I stopped doing that, but I understand the longing to want to look and be like everyone else.

LOSS OF ACCOUNTABILITY

Before I became a clinician I was a staff member in an intensive residential treatment facility. Trevor, African-American, was a ninth grader, one of ten boys in my group. He had a history of school truancy, physical aggression and physical abuse. When he was two and a half years old, his stepfather poured boiling water on his leg because he hadn't cleaned his room. His stepfather was never caught or charged, because after that, he just up and disappeared. Trevor moved in with his grandmother.

I had arrived for my afternoon shift and my supervisor Dan came and told me that Trevor had just had another breakdown where he stormed around because he was asked to turn down his music. He punched a wall and now was in the cool-down room, a room without much in it where kids go when they're being unsafe.

He then said, "I think you should talk to him about his rage at his father."

I was surprised but agreed to it.

There were just a few minutes before lunch as I went down the hall and gently knocked on Trevor's already ajar door. "Can I come in?"

Trevor looked up. "Whatever," he said, which, knowing him, means "yes you can."

I sat down on the chair across from where he was sitting.

"Let me guess," he said with a sarcastic edge. "You want to talk to me about what happened, right? How I have to control my body and all that other stuff, right?"

I held his gaze. Given our time constraints, I got right to the point.

"Actually, I wanted to talk to you about all of this anger that is inside of you all the time. I think a lot of this is about what your stepfather did to you." Trevor's face became stony and in that moment he looked much older than 15.

"I will never forgive him for what he did to me. And, if I ever see him, I will kill him. He has no idea who he's dealing with."

His arms were shaking and his fingers flickered as if he wanted to make a fist but didn't.

I started to speak but thought better of it.

He leaned forward, engaged.

"Katie, I will be angry at him until the day I die."

Then he exhaled and sat back ever so slightly. His arms relaxed.

All I said was, "Okay."

Dan's intuition was right. Trevor wanted and needed to go there. It was the beginning of an important conversation that we continued through the three weeks he was there. But in that conversation his anger was all that he had. He probably would never see him again. Trevor wanted and needed to hold his stepfather accountable and couldn't.

Whether there was abuse, or not, there's a lot that adopted teens wish they could say to their birth parent and caretakers.

"I hate you."

"I love you."

"How could you do this to me?"

"How could you mess up your life like this?"

"How could you just leave me on the side of the road?"

"Don't you care about me at all?"

For adopted teens justice and accountability is an inaccessible privilege.

TEENHOOD

Adoption and teenhood are inextricably intertwined.

Physical changes include growth spurts, weight gain and acne along with facial hair and voice changes for boys and periods for girls. When teens look more mature and sexually developed, they're viewed differently, an experience which can be a mixed bag. In addition, sexual stereotypes and expectations come into play in the form of pressure and identity confusion. Some adoptees already feel like a stranger to themselves because they look and feel so different from their adoptive family. When they morph into this more mature being, they can feel even more lost and out of place.

Jessica was an eighth grader, adopted from Guatemala, who had been struggling to find her place in her new more developed body.

> *"Maybe I wasn't wearing the right bra or something, but my friend and I were running on our track at school Saturday morning. There was this old guy and he was also running on the track. But then, when my friend and I were running, we noticed that he stopped on the side to get some water. It seemed like he was staring at us. I told my friend, 'let's go' and we just left because it was kind of weirding us out."*

That man might have been leering at them or just taking a water break. But Jessica hadn't had to think about herself as a sexual being before. And, even if that's not what was happening then, it's a reality that she will have to contend with.

Even if they're not sexually active the idea of sex is evocative for adopted teens in two ways. For many adopted teens, their child by birth if they have one at some point will be their first known biological relative. There can be a longing to offer a newborn all of the continuity and care that they felt deprived of.

They can also now identify with their birth parents in a way that they couldn't before, which is that they are now physically equipped to conceive and give birth to a child. Many birth or biological parents were teenagers at the time of relinquishment. For adoptees to know that they could do the same may scare but also intrigue them. Sometimes adopted teens aren't even aware that they long to feel an emotional connection or intimacy with their birth mother which fuels the desire to have a baby by birth.

Thinking becomes more complex in the teen years. Teens become able think beyond "black and white." With this developmental shift, they're able to contemplate the "what ifs" and other intangible questions and possibilities. Adoptees are already haunted by those unanswerable questions but the teen years bring them to another level.

When adopted teens haven't developed their cognitive complexity, it's important to adjust expectations accordingly.

Samantha was a Russian adoptee, a freshman in high school. Samantha's adoptive parents were frustrated and confused. "I keep telling her that she needs to figure out what she's doing this summer. I don't want her just sitting around texting and complaining all day like she did last summer. That was a disaster," her parents lamented when they came in for a consultation.

I had had a session with Sam the previous week.

"I just don't think about things like that," she answered, when I asked her about whether she thinks about the future.

Although Samantha was a teen, she hadn't yet learned to think abstractly. Although she experienced many feelings, facts were easier for her to understand. Given that, it made sense why her parents were hitting their heads against the wall waiting for her to initiate a summer plan, or any plan for that matter. Instead, I recommended that they offer her three options for the summer that she could choose from. If Samantha didn't or couldn't make the choice, her parents would make the decision.

As teens expand and develop their thinking they may also have the perception that they are the center of not just their world but everyone's. Their angst is that no one has ever gone through what they have, no one can understand and no one has it worse than they do. For adopted teens though, there's some truth in those feelings. Being an adoptee can be challenging and different in ways that are hard for others to understand or put into words.

In adoption *and* teenhood, establishing an identity is an important but daunting task, and at times elusive. Generally, teens are emotionally porous. They're influenced by family along with peers and culture. *Adopted* teens, however, are influenced by their adoptive family and by any other families and caretakers they've had on this journey. Those families are alive and well in their psyche as they look towards young adulthood, whether they're known or imagined.

Generally, teens are challenged to become independent and self-sufficient, which means that they can support themselves emotionally and financially. That's a slippery process. One minute they seem more mature than you thought possible and the next they're melting down in ways that you haven't seen in years. Adopted teens feel pulled in opposite directions. On one hand, they know that it's time to grow up. On the other hand, to distance from the care that they endured so much to get feels counterintuitive. To try to depend less on their adoptive parents is difficult because they feel more lost and alone, but is comforting because it suggests that they can take care of themselves.

THE PATH: FOUR SKILLS

It's painful to ponder the ways in which your adopted teen may struggle. It takes a lot of courage for adopted teens to navigate their life. It also takes courage for you to pave their way. The truth is, they need you, a lot. And, just as they face certain developmental tasks, so do you. Those tasks are reflected in these four skills—unrescuing, setting adoption-sensitive limits, having connected conversations and helping them to envision their future.

In some ways you're starting from scratch. When they were younger, it was about comfort and learning and structure. Now, it's about preparing them for the future, for adult relationships and responsibilities, and staying connected for the long haul. As we work on these four skill sets, try to be honest and kind with yourself. To help your family meet their potential, you'll need to know more about yourself— your buttons, vulnerabilities, strengths, fears and relationship tendencies. Remember, being honest with yourself is half the battle.

Chapter 2

The Learning Stance

Donna and John were intelligent, loving, thoughtful parents who had domestically adopted Eileen as an infant. Now a senior in high school Eileen was struggling. She told her parents that she didn't feel comfortable with most of her peers. She was struggling to stay afloat academically. After a long string of snow days in Boston, Eileen told her parents the following morning that she just couldn't get herself to go to school. That's when her parents reached out to me for help.

They were at their wits' end during our first parent guidance meeting.

> *"We've tried everything. I don't know what else to do. Is this an adoption thing? Maybe she's right and she just can't do it. I don't understand."*

Being an adopted teen brings with it multiple layers of loss. But what does being an adoptive parent bring into the mix? I believe that the experience of being an adoptive parent is challenging in its own right. Everything from the decision you made to become an adoptive parent to your parenting decisions can feel as if they're under the microscope.

For example, adoptive parents Judy and Nathan, both Caucasian, described the experience of feeling judged in public with their 12-year-old daughter Charlotte, adopted from Guatemala.

> *"When she has a meltdown while we're at a restaurant I feel like we're just perpetuating the stereotype. I mean, they're already looking at us. I can almost hear the other parents saying, 'See, that mom has no idea how to handle her' or even worse, 'adopted kids are emotional wrecks.'"*

Along with the stigma and stereotypes that surround adoption, adoptees and parents, there's much else that's out of your control including genetic predisposition and previous events in your adopted teen's life.

With so many outside forces, I find that it's easy for some adoptive parents to lose track of their impact on their teen's lives. And, when that happens, they also miss an opportunity to play an active role in making needed changes in the family.

I've known and worked with all kinds of families. Many have improved their lives and lived up to their potential but some haven't. And why not? In my experience, it wasn't solely because of adoption issues or genetic predisposition. It was because adoptive parents didn't change. They continue to view the issue as one with their adopted teen not with them. And, when things don't improve, they hold the teen responsible without seeing their role in the situation. I would suggest that, to some degree, every issue with your adopted teen is a family issue.

Let's return to Eileen's school refusal. On the surface, Eileen was unable to make it to school and needed to go. Eileen was responding to her fears of growing up and separating from her adoptive parents, which may have overwhelmed her. There's truth in that.

But that was just the tip of the iceberg.

Eileen's mother, Donna, was raised in an abusive, dysfunctional household and had been clinically depressed for the past ten years. There were days when she didn't get out of bed and Eileen got herself up, made her own lunch and walked to school, even as a little girl. At one point, Eileen became concerned that her parents were going to get a divorce and worried that if she left home after high school graduation, they would completely unravel.

Donna needed to take more steps to intervene with her depression and she and Nathan needed to take steps to improve the stability of their marriage. They also needed to be more careful not to put Eileen in the middle of their squabbles, forcing her to take sides.

Understanding your adopted teen is important. But understanding yourself in relation to your teen might be even more important. Often, our greatest strength is also our greatest liability. For example, if you are a natural at empathizing, understanding and comforting, you may find it challenging to set firm limits and boundaries. Or, if you are really adept at attending to smaller details of schedules or projects, you may have difficulty seeing the bigger picture.

It's not easy to take a good honest look at yourself. Dwelling too long and hard on who you *aren't* and what you're not doing can make you feel helpless and inadequate. By the same token, continually patting yourself on the back for all that you know can lead to a false sense of security.

HIGH IMPACT

Your impact on your adopted teens' lives outweighs their peers, teachers, crushes, therapists and, yes, even their birth parents.

Specifically:

1. You can hurt their feelings without even realizing it. I'm not talking about those unavoidable times. I'm referring to those "unforced errors" (to use a tennis term) when you hurt their feelings unprovoked.

2. You can inadvertently project your feelings onto your adopted teen. You may attribute a feeling to your adopted teen which is actually yours not theirs.

3. You try to change your teen and lose sight of what you could do differently.

How do I know this? Adopted teens have told me, again and again. They care what you think of them, how you talk about and to them. They predict with startling accuracy how you will react, what you'll say and why. They know you better than you realize. They don't let on because they don't want you to know. It embarrasses them to care so much about how you perceive them. They don't want you to know that they need you. It makes them feel like a little kid, which is the last thing they want.

Many years ago, I worked as a staff person at a residential treatment facility in a camp setting. It was a camp for children and teens with intense emotional and behavioral issues, including physical aggression, rage, attentional issues, anxiety and learning disabilities. In our role as staff members, we spent a lot of time with our group of seventh-grade boys, basically from early morning through bedtime. We went with them to each activity, meals, everything. We knew their history, their treatment plan and their goals. We knew more about them than they knew about us.

But by the time that five-and-a-half-week program was wrapping up, in certain ways, the boys in our group knew us in ways that we didn't know ourselves. Ben, one of the boys in the group, was having difficulty staying calm in soccer and we ended up having to take a break from the activity in order to calm down. We sat down on a log a few feet away.

I started to speak.

Ben said, "Let me guess. You're going to say, let's figure out what happened. If you can't control yourself then we're going to have to take another time out and this time it might be even longer."

I raised my eyebrows. "Are you telling me that you've been listening this whole time?"

"I guess you could say that," he said, flashing a quick smile.

If Ben could know me this well after five and a half weeks, you can only imagine how well your adopted teen knows you.

HURT FEELINGS

"I bruise like a peach!"

Meg, 14 years old, adoptee from Kazakhstan

Cassie, adopted junior in high school, was increasingly withdrawn at home and less motivated in school. Her mother was concerned that she was depressed and got in touch with me. By this session, she had been coming to see me for five months. Her long straight blonde hair was pulled into a low messy ponytail. She wore jogging pants and a sweatshirt.

She often smiled even when she was unhappy and typically didn't display much emotion.

For the first half of the session, Cassie talked about friends, academics and sports. But I had the feeling that she was avoiding something.

"What else has been going on?" I asked, wanting to be serious but inviting.

She breathed in, looked away, then burst into tears. "My mom and I got into a fight!"

I said, "Oh no! What happened?"

Cassie brushed away her tears saying, "She's been really hard on me with schoolwork lately. I got one B and she's saying that I'm not studying enough. During finals week I was really overwhelmed trying to figure out how to organize my time and told her I needed her help."

Cassie stopped crying and fiddled with her ponytail.

"She said that I have to learn how to do this myself because I'm not always going to have her around to bail me out. And, the worst part?"

Cassie started to cry again.

"Her chair scraped my leg when she got up. She didn't even notice! There was blood all over the place!"

We've talked about many difficulties but it was her rift with her mother that brought her to tears.

"Maybe we could talk with your mom about it?" I suggested. "She could join our session next week. Let her know how you're feeling?"

Cassie replied, "There's no way. She'll just tell me that I'm being too sensitive or melodramatic. Trust me. It won't make a difference."

Cassie may have exaggerated her leg injury but her feelings were real. She feared that if we had a family meeting, her mom would view Cassie as the problem and not see her own role in the conflict. Her mom may have viewed this as just one of many tiffs that they'd had over the years, but for Cassie, it cut a little deeper.

MISPLACED FEELINGS

"I'm worried about my daughter Sarah," Debbie said. She was one of six in my group for parents of adopted teens. Her daughter and only child was headed off to college in the fall.

The others nodded supportively.

"I think she'll be lonely. I don't want her to feel abandoned, like I don't want her here. She has no idea what it's going to be like."

Debbie shifted in her chair. She thought for a second then grinned.

"Sarah says whenever I come back from an adoption workshop I ask her if she feels abandoned. She rolls her eyes and says 'not this abandonment stuff again Mom!'"

The others chuckled. Another mom said, "I do the same thing!"

"How *does* Sarah feel about college in the fall?" I asked.

"Great! No problem at all! She can't wait!"

"So, who is worried about feeling abandoned again? Is it you or her?"

Debbie threw her head back laughing. "You're right. It's me! I'm not ready! I feel abandoned! I don't want her to go!"

Therapists often describe this as projection, when a person inadvertently projects their feelings onto another person. People do this to defend against being overcome by their own emotions. It's not uncommon, probably something we've all been guilty of at one time or another. It's often subtle and can go unrecognized and unaddressed. And, when you continue to assign a feeling to your teen that is really yours not theirs, your teen may resent feeling caught in something that they can't describe.

The result of an unchecked projection can be similar to that of Chinese handcuffs, a small toy that is a little tube a few inches long made out of straw. You put one finger in each end and the goal is to pull them back out. The trick is that if you try to pull them both out at once it contracts in a way that it's impossible to extricate yourself. But if you just pull out one finger without the other, the "handcuffs" come off immediately. This is also true with projections.

Let's think about Debbie again. If she hadn't recognized that she was projecting her fears about college onto Sarah, she might have gone home and pressed her daughter about being scared about college. Her daughter undoubtedly would have denied it.

Debbie might have continued, "Sweetie, it's okay to be nervous. College is a huge thing. Why wouldn't you be nervous about something like that!"

To which her daughter might become increasingly annoyed and eventually snap at her mom. Debbie would think that her daughter was moody and not owning her anxiety. I challenge you to pull back first to avoid being trapped in a never-ending cycle.

I did that to my daughter, Chloe, too. My parents don't travel like they used to and we see them less often. Chloe has a special bond with my mother and they make the most of their time together. Chloe was tearful when it was time to say goodbye. Later that evening, I said to my husband, "Chloe was really upset to see Mom go." Chloe? True, but I was upset, too. I had inadvertently used Chloe's feelings to hide my own. Chloe read this section of the book and said, "Yeah, you were crying, too!" I was hoping that she had somehow missed that, but yes. I'd be a fool to deny it anymore. There's no proof; you just have to see it.

FAULTY MODELING

I was bowling with my husband and kids who were four and seven at the time. I was heading back to our lane with the pizza we'd ordered. I noticed a father with his two boys a few lanes down. While the father was taking his turn, the boys started arguing and the older one ended up shoving the younger one who shoved him right back.

The father stormed back to the seats, grabbed the older son's arm and got in his face, fast and furious. "Did you just push your brother? Don't ever do that again, do you hear me!"

Do as I say, not as I do.

This father told his son not hit his brother and yet his tone and body language were equally aggressive. The parent sets the tone. For the boys to stop, the father would also need to stop. I worried that the father would continue to blame the boys for their behavior as opposed to recognizing and addressing his role in the problem.

Now, just to be clear. You've likely influenced your adopted teen in countless positive ways as well. Faulty modeling is considered to be anything that parents do, say or believe that they don't want for their teen. For example, if your adopted teen is extremely self-critical could it be possible that you're role modeling that in some form or another?

My daughter loves the tooth fairy. When she was seven years old, she wrote the tooth fairy a note and put it under her pillow. I asked her if I could read it first. She said, "No, it'll just upset you."

I read it later.

Dear Tooth fairy,

I'm sorry my tooth doesn't look very good. If you don't want to give me anything I'll understand. I'll try to make the next one better.

From, Chloe

Where was she getting this? Had I been too critical with her? Was I role modeling that it better be perfect or else? Not in a way that was extreme or severe but who we are is undeniable. After a period of palpable guilt at what I had done to her, I started trying to send a different message, less perfectionistic, more accepting. I don't doubt that there were other factors such as temperament and the culture of our town. But my part was something I could change, so why not start there?

THE LEARNING STANCE

Taking responsibility for your role and accessing your vulnerability are the keys to successfully moving forward. You'll better understand your impact on your adopted teen and pave the way into young adulthood, exactly what they need from you right now.

VULNERABILITY

Jack, early forties, foster parent of 12-year-old Dorian, had been coming in to see me for over a year. Jack planned to adopt Dorian and contacted me so that Dorian could have the emotional support he needed to make the transition.

We all met weekly for about a year before the big day in court that made it official. I saw them later that same day in my office for their weekly session and asked about how it had gone.

His father answered, "Best day of my life. I'm the happiest guy in the world." He wasn't one to smile much, but through his coarse voice, his words were heartfelt. There was a lot of love there.

His son looked away.

"Dorian? What about you?"

He shrugged and slightly shook his head, shuffling his feet, as if he was trying to share his father's joyful mood, but couldn't somehow.

"Fine," Dorian muttered.

I had worked with Dorian long enough to know that his feelings about his biological family were complicated. His biological father disappeared when he was four years old. His mother was a heroin addict. Jack had been his foster parent for over two years. He had come to love and trust him.

But he wished for a long time that his biological family would come back together. And, when his adoption became official, it also signaled the end of his hope. He needed time to grieve, to come to terms with that loss. Dorian was feeling rejected, alone and even guilty that he was interfering with his father's joy.

In the midst of his joy, Jack had inadvertently lost sight of Dorian's pain.

I spoke to it. "Jack, this is a huge day and for you, it's the beginning of something. But for you Dorian, it's also the end of something. There's loss in it, too. I know how hard it's been to deal with everything that happened with your biological family. To know that they weren't able to make it work is difficult. There's a lot of sadness in it."

Dorian looked back at me, as if to agree.

Dorian was feeling vulnerable and alone. I wanted Jack to access his own vulnerability in order to help his son.

"Jack, I want to ask you something. How did you decide to become an adoptive parent?"

I wanted to draw out any feelings that would potentially overlap with what Dorian was going through.

"I wasn't getting any younger. Wasn't in a relationship. Decided that I wanted to have a family."

I tried again.

I leaned in, making direct eye contact. "Yes, but what about that moment, though, *before* you had decided? There must have been a moment before you knew what you were going to do? Tell me about that moment."

Jack narrowed his eyes back at me like a standoff. He had a tough exterior; he was not one to wear his heart on his sleeve. I maintained his gaze.

He rolled his eyes, then said, "My father died. I didn't want to be the end of the line."

Dorian looked at his father.

"And, you felt alone," I continued. "It was hard to imagine your future."

"Yes."

"It was a difficult time for you."

"Yeah it was. I didn't know what I was going to do. Then I realized that I really wanted to have a family. I contacted Department of Children and Families and met Dorian here. Now here we are." He reached out and squeezed his son's shoulder.

Jack's response helped in a myriad of ways. The fact that Jack decided to access his own vulnerability helped Dorian to feel less alone and exposed. It provided depth to Jack's joy and a history to their family.

YOUR MOVE

Amanda was in my parent group. She and her husband Jeff adopted their daughter Lissa from foster care after a year of infertility. Lissa was five years old when she joined their family. Amanda reported that everything went smoothly until her freshman year in high school when Lissa started sneaking out of the house, at which point their relationship with her rapidly deteriorated.

"She barely says two words to me at this point. It's been like this for over a year," Amanda said flatly, in our group meeting with five adoptive moms gathered in my office.

"Last week we went to a funeral for a distant cousin of mine. I really thought it would be a great opportunity for us to talk about adoption and loss. But when I tried to talk with her she just told me to shut up and stalked off."

The others nodded empathically.

She furrowed her eyebrows. "All of the books tell you not to wait for them to bring up adoption stuff so they know that it's okay to talk about it."

I replied, "When they were younger, maybe, but the teen years are different. For teens, issues in adoption and loss are so personal and private. It takes a lot of courage and trust to get into those topics and even then it's difficult to talk about."

"Remember what it was like when you were in the midst of your infertility treatments? Do you remember what it was like to talk about that with others in your life? Not easy, probably. It's the same with adoption. And, if things aren't going well between the two of you, that's even more reason not to go there. You can only do that after you're already more connected, not as a *way* to connect."

Amanda looked intrigued. "So you're saying that I shouldn't ask her about adoption."

"As a first step, yes. If you really need to share your thoughts about adoption and loss, don't do it in question form. Let's say it's her birthday, for example. Instead of asking Lissa whether she thinks about her birth mother, you could talk about how you think about her birth mother on her birthday. That way she doesn't feel put on the spot but can have the option to respond."

The following week, Amanda gave us the update.

"I did what you said. I didn't ask her any questions. The only thing I said as we were passing through her half-sister's old neighborhood was, 'This is where your half-sister used to live. I wonder how she's doing,' and then just left it at that. She didn't say anything then, but I felt empowered about how I had handled it."

"Then," Amanda continued, "on the ride home, she talked almost the whole time! She talked about soccer and summer camp but still! It was a thirty-five minute ride. I couldn't believe it."

Amanda had spent months trying to open up the lines of communication. But when she opted to respond differently, the shift was immediate. It was the first of many important steps in the right direction.

LOOKING IN THE MIRROR

- What are your strengths as an adoptive parent?

- What are your blind spots?

- How can you respond differently to your adopted teen in a helpful way?

Chapter 3
The *Unrescue* Mission

You've probably heard of those sea turtles that hatch at certain times of the year on the beach. I've never seen them up close but their journey compelled me. They are the quintessential underdogs, so vulnerable but determined. I read that it's best not to intervene even though they seem like they need our help. When people pick the little guys up and carry them across the beach to place them in the sea, it doesn't help them. In fact, it compromises their chance of survival. That extended walk from the beach to the sea serves a purpose. It builds strength that they will need later. They're not helpless. They're survivors.

Like the turtles, if you rescue your adopted teen too much, life will be harder for them down the road. Metaphorically speaking, do you pick up your adopted teen when it's in their best interest to walk?

The dynamic of rescuing in your relationship with your adopted teen can be powerful, nuanced and often problematic. Typically, rescuing refers to the act of saving someone (or something) from a dangerous or distressing situation. But for our purposes, it's more than that. It is the potential dynamic in the relationship between adoptive parent and teen, in which adoptive parents tamper with or intervene in life experiences that cultivate the ability to adapt and cope with adversity.

Andrea, an adoptive mother, struggled with how to stop rescuing her daughter.

> *"She has learning disabilities and gets really overwhelmed by school. She's always been pretty anxious. At one point, she just stopped doing her homework for one of her classes. I used to step in and talk to the teachers. I was her biggest advocate, really. I went in with my big binder and just went at it. But I don't know how to help anymore. She told me to stay out of it but she's failing two classes! I told her to go see the teacher for help. She agrees but then doesn't follow through. It breaks my heart to see her doing this to herself."*

When you attempt to rescue your adopted teen from their emotional distress, you're not just saving them (and yourself) from further heartache and tension. You're blocking the opportunity for them to learn and grow. Imperfection and even failure are effective teachers. Learning to tolerate life when it could be better will ultimately enable your adopted teen to feel good about themselves and give them the tools they need for that all-important transition into young adulthood. Experiencing failure will also, down the road, strengthen your relationship with them as well.

For adoptees, being saved or rescued was a part of their narrative. They were in an emotionally and/or physically damaging situation that might have threatened their survival. Adoptees had no power or control in what happened next. By no fault of their own, most adoptees did need rescuing earlier in life. They were nearly casualties of a traumatic situation and dependent on the kindness of strangers. Being the victim of a toxic family situation was likely something they'd just as soon forget but it's complicated. That need to be rescued has become familiar. In my experience, adoptees find themselves drawn to it, perhaps in an attempt to work through and synthesize the adoption experience. But needing to be rescued is also the scariest feeling in the world because it suggests that they have no voice, no power and no sense of agency.

Delia was 13 when she started taking the train home. On rainy or snowy days, her mother, Sandy, told her that if she could she would pick Delia up from her dance class. The first few times it happened, Delia called her mom at home to come to pick her up. The following week, Sandy told Delia that she would be at a doctor's appointment when her dance class finished and wouldn't be able to pick her up.

Her daughter was furious. "Didn't you see the weather today? You said that you'd pick me up when it rains!"

Her mom apologized. "I'm so sorry, sweetheart. I made this appointment months ago."

Her daughter rolled her eyes. "Great. Thanks a lot. So much for being there for me!" And, with that, she blew out of the house in a huff.

Sandy felt terribly guilty and unsure if she had done the right thing. On one hand, she didn't want to renege on what she had already said. She was clear with Delia that it wouldn't be every time. On the other hand, Sandy feared that maybe she hadn't been sensitive enough to the possible abandonment issues that could have been triggered. Maybe it wasn't fair to ask that of her, Sandy worried. She feared that she had potentially damaged her relationship with Delia. After all, she thought, it was already strained between them. Have I just made things even worse?

Sandy's anguish isn't uncommon. It's difficult to figure out when to step in and when to step back. Obviously, this is not just a potential issue for adoptive parents but for all of today's parents. It overlaps the helicopter parent, enabling, pampering and overprotecting. To complicate matters, the decision is not black and white. One family's rescuing is another family's everyday parenting. To some degree, it's a judgment call, but the stakes feel uncomfortably high.

For adoptive parents, the rescuing dynamic may be more directly linked to adoption. Adoptees may at times feel humiliated, deprived and abandoned. Over time, adoptive parents become increasingly aware that they cannot fully compensate for the hardship of their son or daughter's past. Because they can neither prevent nor completely understand their adopted teen's pain, the pull to rescue may be even more compelling.

Are you a rescuing parent? Do you think you would you pick up those baby turtles and bring them right over to the water's edge? You wish that you could take away their pain, but in times of clarity, know that it hurts them in the long run.

One adoptive father said about his 17-year-old adopted son, who was failing most of his classes and at risk of not graduating, "If I can make his life easier for him why wouldn't I do that?" Perhaps you can resonate with the following statements and others that I've heard over the years. He's been through so much already. I just want her to be happy all the time. I just couldn't ground her. Her friends are all that she has. I couldn't let him make a mistake like that. I never ever want her to feel abandoned.

Rescuing can take many forms. The classic rescue is when your teen calls with an unexpected urgent demand of you. And, if you don't do it, things are not going to be okay, according to them, at least. There are variations to that theme. You may find yourself rescuing them from a place such as school because they're not feeling well or a summer program that wasn't what they expected. Sometimes parents rescue their teen by not holding them accountable. Examples include expecting too little of them at home with chores such as dishes or laundry. Or perhaps you end up helping them too much with their research paper or exam to make up for their lack of preparation and time management.

Rescuing may become more extreme as the stakes are raised. One of my very first cases in the Emergency Department (ED) at Children's Hospital was an example of this dynamic. My role in the ED was to conduct psychiatric evaluations, which meant that I made decisions about if and whether a higher level of care was necessary such as a psychiatric hospitalization.

When I arrived, the family had been there for a couple of hours. Lizzy, an adopted 15-year-old girl, had made a suicide attempt by swallowing a bunch of pills and was brought in by her parents. When I arrived for the beginning of my shift she was getting her stomach pumped with charcoal to remove the toxins that she had ingested. Clearly, Lizzy needed to be psychiatrically hospitalized.

But Lizzy's parents, Hannah and Jeff, were against it.

"We just want to take her home. She just needs to be at home with us," Hannah said, teary eyed.

I responded, calmly, "This is very serious. Your daughter just made a suicide attempt. She needs to be in a place that can ensure her safety and provide the help that she needs."

"I know," Hannah replied, "but this was a wake-up call for us and for her. We'll get her the help she needs. Besides," she added, "we adopted Lizzy when she was five years old and the last thing we want is for her to feel abandoned. We just can't let that happen."

It was true that Lizzy might feel abandoned if she was hospitalized. But *being* abandoned and *feeling* abandoned are two very different things.

Being abandoned is a tragic situation that no child deserves.

But feeling abandoned is natural and, I would argue, a necessary part of growing up.

Hannah and Jeff weren't able to face the truth that, although they would always be her parents, they couldn't keep her safe. They were overcome with their fears about their daughter, about themselves as parents and the meaning of what had happened. Of course, this is an extreme situation. But even in smaller situations, adoptive parents worry about causing further damage to their teen's self-esteem, their relationship and their ability to function in their everyday life.

There are other ways in which the adoption narrative may reinforce the rescuing dynamic. You became an adoptive parent after your teen's birth parents couldn't. You picked up where they left off. That's how the narrative goes. You were the one who didn't abandon them and will stick by them from now on. And, although you probably didn't rescue them in a literal sense, it is an aspect of your role. The opposite of rescuing is abandoning. You may also feel caught in this paradigm. To make decisions that may threaten your role as the good one may not feel like a worthwhile risk to take.

I often work with adoptive parents who experienced significant trauma in their families of origin such as abuse, alcoholism and neglect. Understandably, they don't want their children to suffer the way that they did growing up. And, while it allows parents to better empathize with their adopted teens, it can also leave them at risk for overcompensating and overprotecting.

THE COST

Rescuing your adopted teen from their life comes at a cost. When adopted teens are constantly rescued they can often become more entitled, critical, less adaptive and more perfectionistic. This dynamic may over time compromise your relationship and interfere with your adopted teen becoming a responsible young adult. Your teen is so used to the implicit agreement that your job is to make everything okay that they've come to expect it. And, when things don't go their way, they hold you responsible.

How does the rescuing dynamic compromise the wellbeing of your adopted teen?

It can lower their ability to tolerate and cope with feelings that may be rooted in adoption, such as feeling abandoned and rejected. The process of building "emotional immunity" includes exposure. Avoiding that exposure is counterproductive. The way that you respond, however, can make all the difference.

Feeling rescued can breed anxiety for adopted teens. They can sense that their parents are worried or even panicked, which holds meaning for them. It may convey to them that life is scary and overwhelming. Or it may also suggest that you lack of confidence in them. The teen is thinking, "Well, if my dad is pulling me out of this, he must not think I can handle it. Maybe I really can't!" It becomes a self-fulfilling prophecy. They feel less competent and more dependent on you and that scares them. One of their greatest fears is that ultimately they won't be able to make it on their own.

In the rescuing dynamic, everyone ends up feeling disempowered to some degree. Adopted teens often perceive their role as the victim of someone or something. This means that the blame and responsibility is on another and that they lack a sense of agency in the matter. But you might also feel like a victim of your adopted teens' entitlement and demands. It may feel like a lose-lose situation. If you give in, you feel like you're enabling it, but if you say no, you've instigated an emotionally charged confrontation.

NEXT STEPS: FROM RESCUING TO EMPOWERING

Judging whether a situation is a rescue or an assist is to some degree in the eye of the beholder. That said, shifting from rescuing to empowering is an important step in the right direction.

Being empowered is the opposite of being a victim. You always have a choice and those choices are a source of power. In fact, when I talk with adopted teens, I use those words to reinforce that concept: "So, you chose not to complete your homework assignment," or "You chose to take the car without permission."

These guidelines will focus on the classic rescue, which is when your teen contacts you in a panic with an unexpected urgent request or demand of you, but will hopefully be relevant to other forms of rescuing as well.

Let's say that your teen forgets to print out their paper due for school and is now frantically texting or calling asking you to go home, print it and bring it over to school right away. For the sake of argument, let's say that you work 45 minutes away. In order to do this, you would have to take the rest of the day off.

Making the decision

Is this a rescue? And, do you say yes or no?

To make an informed and swift decision, ask yourself these questions:

- *Is this an exception or a pattern?* If this is the third time this month that they've called you to bring something of theirs to school, it's a pattern. But if it's really a favor or they are someone who doesn't usually ask for help, it might be worth rearranging your schedule.

- *How can my teen gain the most from this experience?* If you step back and allow life to happen, they will have the opportunity to work on managing stress, problem solving and disappointment. But you may decide that they could learn just as much with your help.

- *If I say yes, will it happen more often?* You know your teen and their tendencies pretty well. Are they someone who has to learn the hard way? Adopted teens often learn more from what *did* go wrong than from what *could* go wrong.

- *Am I feeling manipulated, angry or taken for granted?* Being attentive to your own feelings can also help you to make an informed decision. If you are feeling resentful and angry there's probably a legitimate reason why.

- *What are my fears if I say no?* Acknowledging and exploring what you are afraid of will help you see them for what they are: worst-case scenarios. Your teen needs you not to base your decisions on what could go wrong but on what's right.

- *If I say yes, will they appreciate what I've done for them?* This is another way to gauge where your teen locates responsibility. If he holds you responsible, he won't be too appreciative because he'll take you for granted. But if he holds himself responsible he'll likely be more appreciative.

- *What would an empowered parent do?* Asking this question can sometimes give you the clarity that you need. It's not always realistic to do what's best. You might surprise yourself.

Decision tip: try to buy some time. It's natural to be pulled into their timetable, but if at all possible, try to give yourself a few minutes to make a clear-headed decision. You could do that by not texting back right away, or just telling them that you'll look at your schedule and let them know in a few minutes. Often parents react and then look back and wish that they had taken more time. Taking that few minutes will give you a better chance of responding, not reacting. If they rush you, just say, "You're on one time schedule but I'm on another. You just called me and I need a few minutes in order to figure it out what's possible."

Communicating your decision

Let's say that you decide not to leave work, print and bring your teen's paper to school.

Parents have many different ways that they tell their teen "no."

- A *burdened* response leads with resentment and, in some ways, victimhood.

    Example:

    "I shouldn't have to stop everything just because you forgot your stuff, which is your responsibility by the way.

I told you to put out your stuff the night before but you didn't. Now you realize why that was so important."

Your teen might respond by saying something like, "Well, maybe you could be a better parent and get me those binders when you said you would and I wouldn't have this problem."

With this response, you've inadvertently stooped down to their level. I often tell parents never to get down in the dirt with their teen. Then it becomes a blame game, one which they're extremely skilled at.

- There's also the *flippant* response. This happens when you're trying not to get pulled in but end up going to the other extreme.

  Example:

  "Oh, well, I guess you're going to have to figure something out! This is your problem not mine." I know that I said that you shouldn't wrestle in the dirt with them but it's also important not to convey that you've washed your hands of them. This response can lead to a complete communication breakdown.

- Then there's the *waffling* response. This is when you don't really give them an actual answer.

  Example:

  "You want me to go and print it then bring it? I don't know, honey. That sounds difficult. It's a 45-minute drive from work. Can't you just explain to your teacher what happened?" You're secretly hoping that if you explain how much they're asking of you, they'll realize that and say, "You're right, Mom. I'll take care of it myself." Instead, what they do is push even harder because they see that you're ambivalent.

- An *empowered* response clearly says yes or no and keeps the focus on them. It avoids blaming, lecturing, patronizing or guilting.

  Example:

  "No, I'm not going to do that. School stuff is up to you."

  Simple, straightforward and to the point. They may initially become angry with you because you said no. Try not to respond too much to their anger or explain why this is better for them in the long run and how you made this difficult decision.

Tip #1: Allow but don't encourage their anger. There are (at least) two ways to understand your teen's anger when you say no to an urgent request/demand. One is that they're feeling desperate and needy. But the other reason is that they may also agree that it's better for you not to get involved and just want to keep up appearances. For that reason, it makes sense not to focus on their anger. So, for example, if they say, "Are you serious? Why aren't you helping? I knew you would do this!" You can just say, "I know you're unhappy about this," and then move on.

Tip #2: Keep empathy to a minimum. Even when saying no to your teen is for the best, it can be difficult for them to hear. Still, making empathic statements can actually worsen the situation. If you say things like, "Oh, I know that you were really hoping that I could do that. It's a really difficult situation. I'm sure it's overwhelming," it actually can promote regression when what we want in that moment is to build coping strategies and the ability to adapt.

Follow-up

The next stage is the follow-up conversation afterwards, after school or later that evening. If things haven't gone well, it's a chance to shift it in a better direction. If things went okay, it's a chance to solidify that progress.

The goal in the follow-up conversation is not to rehash and deconstruct what happened but to finish it. It's often simple and brief.

Here's an example of an ideal follow-up conversation:

Parent: "So what happened today with your paper and everything? Did you end up talking with your professor?"

Teen: "Oh, yeah, I told him what happened and he said that I could just e-mail it to him after school. He didn't care."

Parent: "That's good. Well, good night."

Teen: "Good night."

Things not to say

1. "I know you were disappointed when I said that I couldn't do that."

   Don't bring up how you said no. It just reignites the situation and may expose your guilt about your decision.

2. "Sweetie, that's fantastic! I'm so happy that you decided to talk to your teacher!"

   Stay more neutral. Being positive and encouraging can lead the teen to feel like a younger child.

3. "I know you were mad when I said no, but aren't you glad you figured it out?"

   Don't comment on the fact that they might be secretly proud that they got through it without your intervention.

REMEMBER...

Shifting from rescuing to empowering is essential to making the most of these years. It takes courage to parent in new ways. Of course, you won't always make the best or the most informed decision. The important part is that you're open to learning.

Rescuing is in part about setting boundaries. Those boundaries set the tone for the following chapter about setting limits that are adoption sensitive.

Chapter 4

Setting "Adoption-Sensitive" Limits

The purpose of setting limits is to help adopted teens to make informed decisions and to keep them safe. We're not trying to control them; we're just trying to pave their way. Effective limits convey your values and expectations while holding them responsible for their choices.

Setting effective limits is at its core about embracing your role as an authority in your adopted teens' life. What do you expect of them and why? How have you communicated those expectations? And how do you hold them accountable?

Setting limits and expectations is also very much intertwined with adoption. For example, in the absence of effective limit-setting, your adopted teen may ultimately feel *more* abandoned, not less.

Sandra, adopted from Ethiopia at three months old, was a high school junior when her parents, Becky and Rick got in touch with me. Sandra had snuck out of the house and taken the car without permission more than once. Becky and Rick were angry and felt like they had tried everything, including the addition of certain rules and guidelines, such as no smoking in their car. They informed Sandra that if she or any of her friends smoked in the car than Sandra would lose the car for two weeks.

In her individual session, Sandra reported that in fact she had broken many of their rules including this one. "I've smoked twice in the car this Saturday plus last week after class and before swim practice," she said. It wasn't her rule-breaking that struck me. It was her tone, which was more than sadness. Given that Sandra and her parents often seemed to be in a perpetual battle for power and control, I was fascinated that she wasn't gloating that her parents had done the thing that she said that she wanted, which was to "leave her alone." She would never have wanted her parents to know what she was really feeling, which was despair.

For Sandra, when her parents didn't uphold this rule, it held certain meaning. It suggested to her that her parents weren't reliable, trustworthy. Clearly Sandra was not neglected, but she did feel neglected. Had they forgotten what they had told her, or just didn't care enough to see it through? Maybe they were too scared of how she would react if they held her to it. Why were they walking on eggshells? Sandra might have thought, "If my own parents are scared of me, how will they go up against me if and when they need to? And, what does that say about me then?"

The path to young adulthood doesn't begin with love. It begins with respect. When a teen tells me that they don't respect their parents, I know that that's where our work should begin.

Steven was a domestically adopted freshman in high school. His father Barry worked in finance and mother Julie was a school counselor before she got married. His parents met while attending the same prominent liberal arts school. They adopted Steven at 14 months through a private agency.

His parents contacted me regarding multiple issues. He was smoking cigarettes and marijuana, failing most of his classes, cutting school and having angry outbursts at home. One week earlier he had stormed out of the house because his parents asked him why he wasn't taking school more seriously. His parents ended up calling the police after he didn't return until the following morning.

His parents sighed, "We've talked with him about the importance of school. It goes in one ear and out the other. We would tell him that we're not mad. We just want him to have the opportunities later in life. He doesn't realize how much he's limiting his future. He'll never get a good job if he keeps going this way. I don't know what else to do. It just seems like he doesn't care about his life."

Julie's eyes welled up.

I nodded. "What have the consequences been for him when he does these things?"

They looked at each other quizzically and then back at me.

"Consequences?"

"Yes, you know, what happens to him when he smokes pot in the house or cuts school?"

Barry said, "Well, no, I guess we haven't really. But he knows how upset and worried we are. Anyway, it feels kind of hypocritical. We also smoked pot when we were teenagers so who are we to tell him not to do it?"

Steven's parents successfully provided a loving, safe space, almost "womb-like" atmosphere from the beginning. But when teenhood hit and Steven's troubles ballooned, Barry and Julie weren't actually holding him accountable for his actions. Whether or not they were aware of it they had prioritized love and belonging over respect and trust. In truth, it's respect and trust that has to come first.

Many adoptive parents I've worked with find themselves trying to avoid the daunting task of setting limits. They do this by attempting to collaborate or negotiate with their teen instead of being the authority. Sometimes parents have become so emotionally worn that they simply don't have it in them to say no. Most want to do right by their teen but are confused about how and where to begin. And some parents just don't find it necessary to include guidelines or structure.

Of course, some adoptive parents are the opposite. They are so authoritative and restrictive that their teen barely has a life. This is also problematic. When a teen feels like they have no voice in the family, they feel trapped, and their survival instinct kicks in. They begin to strategize on how to get out of the situation by becoming more self-sufficient. In this situation, adoptive parents find themselves at risk for being "abandoned" by them.

When parents take setting limits and being an authority too far it can become abusive and cruel. I remember talking with an adult adoptee at a conference about this theme of respecting adoptive parents.

She flinched. "My adoptive parents were physically abusive," she said. "My father used to always say that I needed to respect him."

I understood her concern. The task of being respected by your adopted teen is not to control or restrict them. It is to help them to make informed decisions, learning skills that will help them prepare for young adulthood. And strengthen your relationship.

But why might it be challenging specifically for adoptive parents to set limits?

In my experience, many adoptive parents equate saying no with deprivation. It's natural to want to compensate for deprivation that someone has experienced. If a person was starving for extended periods of time, why wouldn't you want to give them a feast?

A few years ago, I saw a little boy for psychotherapy, named Nate, who had been abandoned and left for dead at the age of two. When he started with me, Nate was four years old, newly adopted. He was really cute. His smile lit up a room. And, despite it all, he was basically a happy kid. Once, we heard an ambulance whiz by outside. He looked up, as if this wasn't his first ambulance, quickly regrouped and went back to playing Legos. His speech was delayed and every picture I asked him to draw looked the same—scribbles.

Now, I am really clear about my boundaries but part of me wanted to give him…everything—the rest of the afternoon, snacks and toys to take home. I knew better, of course. From me, he needed a therapist, nothing more, nothing less. My wish to give Nate everything was how I managed my own feelings of helplessness about his trauma. Of course, nothing can alter his past. To think that I could somehow make up for it is an illusion. Unchecked, our wish can be too similar to pity. Pity suggests that we feel sorry for them, which is the last thing that this boy or anyone needs.

Do you worry that when you set limits you're depriving your adopted teen somehow?

But even when you're ready to do right by your adopted teen, how do you set and uphold limits while keeping adoption in mind?

SETTING RESPECTFUL LIMITS

Asserting your authoritative voice

Darby, a single adoptive mother, had that chance to assert her authority. She came in to see me because her 13-year-old adopted daughter Gwen was having meltdowns several times a week. These meltdowns included screaming for extended periods of time as well as, on a couple of occasions, physically kicking or pushing her.

Darby said calmly, shaking her head, "Let's see. Well, just yesterday, she asked if she could go sleep over at her friend's house this Saturday night. I explained that we had her cousin's wedding that evening and that it wasn't a good night for it. She flipped out and started screaming at me. I tried to stay very calm and I just try to take some space and go to my room, but she just followed me screaming at the top of her lungs. I try to tell her to calm down but she just keeps going. It's just the two of us in the family so there's nowhere really to go. We spend a lot of time in close proximity to each other. I want her to know that we're going to be okay."

Offhandedly, she added, "Boy, do I hate it when Gwen says 'shut up' to me. That drives me crazy. That is unacceptable. I don't allow the children I have in my day care to say it and I find it offensive."

Darby had been a nanny for over ten years and ran her own day care. I wanted to activate Darby's more confident, authoritative self.

"So, you're pretty confident at work?"

She nodded. "Yes, I am pretty sure of myself. I know I'm good at my job."

"So you're saying that it's clear to you and to the kids that you're in charge."

"Yes."

"How would you handle it if one of the kids in your day care said 'shut up' to another child?"

Darby didn't skip a beat. "I would stop whatever I was doing, get down on her level, make eye contact with the child and say, 'We do not say 'shut up' in this classroom. That is not how we treat each other. Do you understand?'"

At work, Darby knew that she was in charge and that was evident in her voice.

In her session the following week, Darby told me about a situation with her daughter that began in a familiar way but that ended quite differently. Her daughter was worried that they would be late for her ice-skating lesson because she had stayed after school to get homework assignments that she had missed from the previous week of being sick. Her daughter was frantically rushing around trying to gather her things.

Darby said, "Don't worry. We'll make it there if we leave now. Just calm down."

Her daughter yelled back, "Oh, just shut up!"

Darby walked over to her and said, firmly, "Gwen, look at me."

Gwen pretended not to hear her.

Darby repeated, more firmly this time, "Look-at-me."

Gwen looked up, a little surprised that her mom was so steadfast.

Darby then said, just as measured, "You do not say 'shut up' to me, ever. That's unacceptable. Do you understand?"

Gwen paused and then replied, "Okay." They got into the car in silence, but Darby was surprised to see that Gwen was calmer somehow.

Neither said much on the car ride after that, but that was the last time Gwen ever told her mother to shut up.

When Darby found her assertive voice, she was able to focus in on a specific issue about which she felt strongly.

She wasn't ambivalent. She did not waffle. Her body language, her words and her tone of voice were in sync. When they're going in various directions, it shows. For example, if you speak in a higher tone of voice than usual, if you avoid eye contact or include lengthy explanations about how and why you decided what you did, you may signify to your adopted teen that you're unsure you're doing the right thing. When you apologize or dwell on how hard this must be for them, that's a signal, too.

Example:

You sit down next to your teen on the couch and say, "Your dad and I talked a lot last night and we decided that you will be grounded this weekend. I know this isn't what you wanted, and if you're unhappy about this I'm really sorry, but it's something that your dad and I felt that we had to do. We hate this as much as you do but we're just trying to do what's best for you. How is all of this for you? I'm sure it can't be easy."

Or:

You knock on their bedroom door and say, "As we discussed at the beginning of the year, when you cut a class during the week you're grounded for that weekend. I'll let you know when dinner is ready."

Why contracts and adoption don't mix

Behavioral contracts are often used to set expectations, limits and incentives. But for adopted teens and families, I assert that contracts are often ineffective and may even weaken your relationship in three ways:

1. *They undermine your authority.* Adopted teens sometimes view contracts as an aid or a crutch that parents use in order to shore up their authority. One adopted teen

summed it up when he said, "They need a contract to control me." It tells your teen that your voice is not enough. The contract becomes your voice and undermines your authority.

2. *They promote secrecy and deception in your relationship.* Belinda, a client of mine, 14 years old, adopted from China at 13 months, told me about her contract. Her contract said that if she didn't smoke or drink by the time she was 18 years old her parents would give her $2500. By the time Belinda was 15 she had already done both, quite liberally, I might add. Not surprisingly, Belinda opted to withhold this information from her parents. At one point she had an empty vodka bottle in her backpack from a party the day before and worried that her parents might have seen it.

    When I asked if she would ever ask them, she answered, "Are you kidding? I'm not going to incriminate myself!" Incidentally, her parents also suspected that she might have breached the contract, but were hesitant to bring it up with her in case they were wrong. The purpose of the contract was as an incentive but instead perpetuated sneakiness, secrecy and emotional distance.

3. *They reinforce the role that contracts play in your family.* Contracts are already part of the adoption narrative. You signed a contract in order to legally adopt your child. To reintroduce the contract as a parenting tool, especially given that it involves the two of you signing off on it, can inadvertently depict your relationship as more legal than personal.

    And, when adoptive parents and teens are struggling, it can even become a weapon of sorts. In session, an angry adopted teen said, "They only have legal authority over

me until I'm 18. When that day comes, I'm out of here."
It can potentially encourage distance and detachment,
not togetherness and connection.

Hidden costs of negotiating

One of the most common missteps that I see from parents
is negotiating consequences. It undermines your authority
and even more importantly it risks humiliating your adopted
teen. For example, let's say that your teen violates curfew one
too many times and you've told them that they are grounded
for one month. First of all, that is too long to ground them.
See the next tip for more on that. Then your teen starts
negotiating like those in jail do when they try to get their
sentence shortened for good behavior. My, are they persistent!
This begging, demanding and pleading can take up a lot of
airtime during the day and in your relationship. Soon, you
realize that that's the main thing you're talking about. Truth is,
negotiating with your teen is a lose-lose situation. If they get
what they want, you lose their respect. If they don't, they
feel humiliated. The experience of begging can be evocative
for adoptees, even when they're not thinking about it that
way. Adoptees couldn't take family, safety or permanence for
granted. They had to depend on the kindness of strangers
when, really, they only trusted themselves. So when you set
a consequence and then leave the door open to negotiate,
it stirs up those feelings of having to fight for their rights
because no one else will.

I did psychiatric evaluations in the Emergency Department
(ED) at Children's Hospital for three years. There I evaluated
Michael, 11 years old, in the ED. Michael was having
rages where he would punch the wall and threaten to hurt

his parents. His parents didn't feel like they could keep him safe at home.

Michael was also unhappy in the ED. The staff could hear him yelling and complaining from down the hall. He was unhappy with his room, his identity bracelet, the hospital food and that he had to be there in the first place.

When I told the family that Michael would be hospitalized, he was irate. "I don't want to go to a hospital! Just take me home!"

His parents tried to console. "Honey, it'll just be for a few days. There'll be people there who can help us understand what's going on." He would have none of it.

Then I said directly to Michael, "It's not your decision. It's mine."

Michael stopped short and just looked back at me. He was clear that I meant what I said. He stopped screaming and thrashing. In fact, Michael seemed relieved.

Why?

When kids have too much power and control, it overwhelms them. And, they don't feel taken care of. Michael was relieved that this decision was in someone else's hands. Your teen should also not have a say in every decision. Your words should reflect that.

For example, stating is different than requesting. "Billy, I need you to take out the trash on your way out" is different than "Billy, would it be possible to take out the trash before you go?"

TAKING THE STING OUT OF SETTING LIMITS

Donna and Jean were adoptive parents of Peter, 15 years old, from Guatemala. "We're out of ideas," Donna said in the initial consultation.

Jean added, frustrated, "Peter is triple-grounded at this point. First he was grounded for failing his math final. Then he was grounded for missing curfew and coming home at 1 am. Then when we decided to take his phone away, he flipped out. He had a swearing fit and trashed his room which added another week. He's up to a month and a half!"

"What were the expectations for him?" I inquired.

"Well," said Donna, "the deal was that if he got a C or higher than he was in the clear. If he got a C– or D+ then he would be grounded for three days. If he got a D– then four days and if he received a failing grade he would be grounded for two weeks. It's all laid out right here in the contract that he signed." She placed a three-page document on my aged coffee table that we sat around in my office.

As I leafed through the document, Jean said, "He hates us. He really does. He says he doesn't respect us, that when he graduates he's going to move out and that there's nothing we can do about it." She rolled her eyes and put her head in her hands, her voice cracking just slightly.

"We tell him how much we love him. We just worry that this is how it's going to be from now on, that he'll move out and never come back." Donna tensed as she combed her hands through her hair.

Things were in a downward spiral. But they could shift to a more positive direction by changing how they set and uphold limits.

1. *Keep rules simple and straightforward.* First, if you need a contract to keep everything straight, then it's too complicated. For example, Peter could be grounded with no phone for one week if he fails a class, nothing more. Keeping things simple also lessens the chance of excessive arguments and debates about the details. Sometimes parents realize that that's the only thing

they talk about with their teen, and you don't want it to dominate your relationship.

2. *Shorter, time-limited consequences are more effective.* With shorter groundings and other restrictions, it would be easier for Peter then to connect it with the original reason for consequence in the first place. It also gives you more leverage because when the next situation happens, you'll have something to take away. Piling on groundings just dilutes the point. Remember, our goal is not for them to make no mistakes; it's to help them to make informed decisions. If the consequences are quicker, they'll potentially be able to make a different choice.

Shorter consequences are like spraying your cat when he jumps up on the counter. You don't need to soak him. He gets the message that what he's doing is unacceptable.

3. *Never get in the mud with them.* One of the hardest parts of setting limits is that it can become physically aggressive. I've heard so many stories of adoptive parents in a tug of war over the phone or barring the door when their teen threatens to leave, or even standing in front of the car if their teen tries to take it without permission. These scenarios downgrade your status even if you do get or stop whatever it is that you're trying to do.

One of the most important ways to sidestep physical confrontations is to state expectations and consequences ahead of time. That way you remove that shock which can lead to an instinctual fight reaction. Also, it's helpful to have another plan in place. For example, if your teen refuses to give you the phone then you'll cut off their phone from your phone company until they give it up, which is when their consequences will begin.

4. *If possible, use consequences for behaviors that can be proved.*
    For example, adoptive parents will often say to me, "I
    don't care what grades she gets as long as she puts her
    best effort in and she's not doing that!" Murky areas
    like whether or not your teen did their best effort are
    dangerous territory and frequently lead to arguments
    and hurt feelings. Grades are just more concrete and
    don't leave as much room for interpretation.

5. *Don't ask them how or why.* Sometimes parents will ask
    their teen, "How could you do this?" or "What were
    you thinking?" then proceed to tell them why what they
    did was faulty judgment. You may not realize that it comes
    across as critical, but it might. When you say something
    like, "Do you know what could have happened?" the
    emotionally vulnerable adoptee may interpret it to feel
    that you're calling them stupid. Even if in your estimation
    it was foolhardy, it will not help to convey that to your
    teen. Consequences can replace lectures and questions.
    Anger alone is not an intervention.

6. *The place for anger is between the two of you.* When your
    teen says or does something that doesn't warrant
    consequences but that you feel is offensive or entitled
    or hurtful, anger can be effective in emphasizing your
    point. For example, if your teen said, "I couldn't care less
    about what you think," you could absolutely say, "That
    really makes me angry! I don't deserve to be spoken to
    this way!"

7. *Keep love out of it.* Often, parents will tell me that when they
    give consequences, they'll also say, "I love you." This may
    seem counterintuitive but it's really best to keep love out
    of it, verbally, I mean. When you tell them that you love
    them, it actually can make them feel more humiliated.

When I worked at a "camp" for emotionally disturbed kids, my group was the 13-year-old boys. When one of the boys was upset and a staff person approached them, they would usually say something like, "Get away from me," along with some profanity. It's humiliating to be "mothered" when you're already feeling vulnerable. Plus, when you tell them that you love them, they get the message that you are uncomfortable with your anger and theirs.

8. *Strive for consistency.* Being consistent in what you expect and how you hold them accountable gives you credibility and helps to establish new behaviors and habits. For example, if you've decided that curfew is important to you to be followed you need to respond the same way, every time. Smaller lasting changes are better than dramatic changes that aren't realistic. It's best to focus in on one or two limits at a time.

9. *Talking about adoption and setting limits doesn't mix.* Sometimes you'll be setting a limit of some kind and your teen will say something that sounds like adoption such as "I knew you didn't trust me" or "Why don't you just kick me out? Everyone else has." It might be tempting to engage in an in-depth conversation about those issues but I'd advise against it. For example, you might say, "Yes, that's what you're feeling but I'd like to make sure we're clear on your grounding," or whatever limit you're setting at the time. When you convey this, you're sending two messages: "Don't use your adoption to justify or deflect from responsibility" and "It's such an important topic that it deserves its very own conversation, not to be thrown in at the last minute."

10. *Be savvy, not sneaky.* Sometimes parents think that their teen is up to something but can't put their finger on exactly what it is. Or they know but they can't prove it. In my experience you should trust your intuition because it's usually correct. When you don't address it, your adopted teen may perceive you as clueless and will respect you less. But you could bring it up in a respectful, but direct way, by saying something like, "I think you've been taking money out of my wallet. I can't prove it, but that's what I believe." Or, "It just seems like there's something you're not telling me. I don't know for sure but if there *is* something, you need to tell me right now." When they deny it, which they probably will, you could just say, "I could be wrong." Knowing that you're onto them may result in a change in their behavior.

Being savvy is different than being sneaky, though. Parents tell me that they monitor their teen's texts or Facebook profile or secretly search their room. Or parents ask their teen something to catch them in a lie. "I just wanted to see whether he would tell me," they'll say. But sneakiness is faulty role modeling. Your teen respects you less because you're not being above board. Like you, they can also tell when you're up to something. Being more upfront will prioritize integrity. For example, you could just tell them that their bedroom is fair game and will be searched periodically, or that there will be random checks of their cell phone to make sure everything is appropriate and within guidelines. Your teen may not love it, but they will appreciate it.

REMEMBER...

Respect precedes love and belonging. After respect comes trust. I'm not saying that every adopted teen needs extensive limits and consequences. That's not always the answer. But rules and guidelines are a part of life. If they don't respect you, they may have difficulty respecting authority in general. Know that, with any changes, sometimes things can get worse before they get better. Change can cause some upheaval, but that's the key to moving forward.

Chapter 5

Empathy in Conversation

Perhaps you've had the experience of being in a conversation that is going smoothly only to have it somehow fall apart. You're left wondering what happened. At times, it can feel that everything you say just makes things worse. Or, perhaps it's hard just to get a conversation to happen at all.

Talking with adopted teens can be a minefield.

Your adopted teen may not turn to you like they used to. But if and when they do it's because they really need you. Their needs get disguised by their iPads and phones, making those conversations with you appear less important. But often adopted teens don't talk with their friends about being teased, or failing a class or losses related to adoption. They turn to you.

I remember talking with a girl, Natasha, adopted from Guatemala in ninth grade, about her friend group. She was telling me about her BFF (best friend forever) at school.

"We tell each other everything," she said, smiling. "We've been friends forever."

I asked, "Have you talked with her about the feelings and struggles that you've had related to being adopted?"

She thought for a second.

"Well, no, not that stuff."

When talking with your teen about such vulnerable issues such as adoption and race, it's not enough to simply be empathic. It's the *connection* with your adopted teen that we want. In order to successfully make an empathic connection with your teen, they need to feel understood by you. It takes a lot of trust for adopted teens to open up about such personal vulnerable issues. If you're still struggling with setting limits and rescuing, those should take higher priority. So, when it comes to trust, addressing the rescuing dynamic and setting adoption-sensitive limits has to come first. Sometimes adoptive parents make the mistake of pushing for a "heart-to-heart" when they're really struggling in their relationship with you. It's not respectful to ask or expect your adopted teen to talk about personal sensitive matters when you aren't really even getting along.

Making that empathic connection has a myriad of benefits, including strengthening your relationship, helping your adopted teen feel less alone and more empowered in the world and paving the way into young adulthood.

But it doesn't just happen.

Pam was a 15-year-old ninth grader adopted from China who grew up just outside of Boston. Pam had ongoing feelings of loss that she didn't have her birth mother and went with her adoptive father, Jake, to China to look for her but was unsuccessful. When she returned, Pam felt depressed, irritable and isolated. Her grades went from As and Bs to Cs and Ds. That's when her mom Karen contacted me.

At this point, we had been meeting for a few months.

"I tried to talk to Mom about stuff like you suggested, but…" Tears welled up in Pam's eyes as she looked away.

"What happened?" I asked, leaning in slightly.

"Well, like I was talking to her about my feelings about being adopted, and just asking why? Why did my birth mom have to give me up?"

"What did your mom say?"

"She just told me about the one-child policy again. That's what she always does."

Pam spoke softly, her shoulders turned inward.

"What was that like for you?" I asked.

"I don't know. It was like she already had the answer. She knew what had happened so she was fine. I guess I just wanted her not to know…not to be so sure…"

She became quiet.

I said, "Like you. So, your mom had figured it out but you still haven't. Your mom told you the political story, which I'm sure you already knew. But you wanted your story, not what happened in the country, what happened to you."

"Yeah."

"It's something that you live with every day. The 'not-knowing.' You want your mom to know how hard it's been. Of course, you'd want to know that. You deserve to know what happened to you."

Pam's conversation with her mom is what I describe as an empathic miss. For our purposes, an empathic miss is when your teen tries to communicate something to you in a personal conversation and ends up feeling misunderstood. Now, I knew Pam's mom fairly well. I knew that she did feel empathic about her daughter's struggles and was attuned to the potential issues of adoption and race. And, of course, it wasn't for lack of love. But, in that conversation, Karen missed that opportunity to connect.

How? Why?

Three possible reasons:

1. Karen misread her daughter's needs. She responded to the content or facts but not the process. Pam was looking for emotional support, not answers. Although Karen may have been feeling empathically towards Pam's emotional angst, she didn't directly express it with words.

2. Karen may have been responding to her own feelings of helplessness as a parent. Karen couldn't provide the story that her daughter needed and deserved. She may have instinctively gone to what she knew instead of staying with her daughter's emotional anguish.

3. Karen may not have actively recalled her own life experiences that might have provided more insight into Pam's feelings. Remember Jack and Dorian from Chapter 2? After Jack actively recalled his own feelings of loss and loneliness, he was better able to empathically connect with his son's feelings of loss and grief.

My adoption status doesn't guarantee an empathic connection with adopted teens I see. While in certain moments I resonate with certain life experiences or feelings they've had, there are other moments in a therapeutic relationship when I cannot personally relate.

My being an adoptee alters my approach to the topic.

As a new clinician, I met Noah, adopted at seven months from Korea. Now in eighth grade, Noah was caught stealing pencils from a classmate's desk and his math teacher suspected that he might have cheated on the most recent exam. They also told me that Noah hasn't been able to admit to anyone that he stole those pencils even though it was thoroughly documented by multiple sources.

His adoptive parents, Sam and Nicole, said that Noah saw a therapist for a while but that it just fizzled out after a few months. Sam and Nicole believed that Noah never really connected with him and that that was one of his issues. Their intuition told them that adoption issues were in play although they couldn't put their finger on exactly how.

Our first meeting, he told me all about his passion for science fiction, video games and his parents. I acknowledged the stealing and the issues of adoption as possible topics for us. I didn't press it. He wasn't someone who talked about his feelings much.

But just as we were finishing up he looked me and said, "It's nice to talk with someone who really understands me."

His comment surprised me.

I smiled warmly and said, "I'm glad you came. See you next Tuesday."

Why did he feel so understood so quickly?

Certainly, my also being a Korean-adoptee facilitated the connection.

But how I talked with him mattered even more.

This is when I clearly saw that adopted teens don't need their parents to have been adopted. You can still convey a sense of understanding and empathy without having been through it yourself.

MINEFIELDS

It seems simple, but it's not. Adoptive parents often find themselves talking with their teen in ways that prevent the empathic connection.

1. "But sweetie…" When your teen feels stupid, ugly or just unloved, you want them to see the truth. "You're gorgeous. Can't you see that?" Or, "But sweetie, there are so many people in your life who love you." "But sweetie, all your teachers say that you're smart. You just need to

apply yourself." It is an attempt to get your adopted teen to see the positives.

This might surprise you, but sometimes when adopted teens hear "but sweetie," they worry that it's too painful for you to tolerate their suffering. For fear of hurting you more, they may attempt to hide their true feelings from you. You can tell them that they don't have to protect you until the cows come home but the "but sweetie" sends another message, which says, "Yes, your emotional pain is too much to bear which is why I keep trying to argue against it."

There's another way that "but sweetie" is problematic. When you continue to disagree with them and try to get them to see the error of their ways, they can end up feeling more inadequate. Instead of feeling reassured, they might instead feel, "Why is this so easy for my parents to see and so hard for me? What's wrong with me?"

2. "We love you and will never abandon you." Sometimes an adopted teen I'm working with might say, "If my mom says she loves me one more time, I don't know what I'll do," or "I know they'll always be there for me but it doesn't help…" Adults put love on a pedestal. We respect, admire and believe in it. But telling your adopted teen how much you love them during times of despair can actually lead them to feel even more guilty knowing that your unconditional love and dedication isn't enough to heal their emotional pain.

There's something else, too. I brought up earlier that the adoption narrative creates a certain dichotomy between you and your teen's birth parent. To the extent that some of the despair might be entangled in feelings about their birth parent, emphasizing the ways that you're different can lead your teen to feel even more fragmented and confused.

3. "I went through the same thing and look at me now."
    Sometimes adoptive parents will share their own story
    of what they went through. Often, their message is
    "See, there's still hope!" Unfortunately, that's not often
    how they internalize it. Often, what they hear is "There,
    there, you'll see what I'm saying when you're older and
    less short-sighted and naïve. It's all going to turn out
    okay." As a result, the adopted teen often feels patronized
    and invalidated. And, they often just feel like you don't
    get it. They want you to be with them not ahead of them.

4. "If…then." "If you would have studied more, then you
    wouldn't have failed math." Parents don't always realize
    why they often criticize, blame or judge. Sometimes it's
    out of anger or frustration on your part. Adopted teens
    may be sensitive to criticism, when they feel that they're
    not measuring up to where you believe they should be.
    The "I told you so," in that message, however unintended,
    can make them feel inadequate and humiliated. In these
    conversations, the goal is not for you to be smarter or wiser.

5. "You poor thing!" There's a fine line between empathy
    and pity. Empathy means that you can understand what
    they're going through. Pity means that you feel sorry
    for them, as if to suggest that there's something wrong
    with them. It also suggests that they're the victim of
    their circumstance, which can be immobilizing.

6. "But this isn't you!" When parents say this, adopted
    teens often feel that you can't accept who they really
    are. When the insinuation for the teen is that they used
    to be different, that also can exacerbate feelings of guilt
    and shame. In attending to your adopted teen's feelings,
    you're also challenged to face your own.

When things aren't going well with their parents, I often get an earful, a rant with specifics, including what the parent did, said, why it was so outrageous and how this makes them respect them even less.

But when that empathic connection was made and the relationship has improved, the adopted teen often has much less to say.

For example: I remember Justin, adopted from India, junior in high school. He told me plainly that he didn't respect his parents and even looked down on them.

"They don't really feel like my parents. They have no idea what I'm going through. They don't understand anything." I led with empathy. I didn't try to convince him how much his parents really did love him, or remind him of how much they had done for him. If I had, he would have likely become further entrenched in his position that they weren't really his parents. Instead I would say, "I could imagine that it might be disappointing to feel like they don't get you." When Justin could see that I wasn't going to doubt him, he began to relax a little. It was like he had been holding his breath and then could finally breathe out.

Two months later, in my session with Justin, we were talking about his break-up with a girl he was really torn up about.

"Have you talked with your parents about it at all?" I asked.

I expected him to say what he typically says: "No, they don't know anything about my life."

But he didn't.

He said, "Yeah, I talked to my mom about it last night."

"Oh, really?"—trying not to seem surprised. "What did you tell her about it?"

He said, "Pretty much everything."

"How was that?"

"It was helpful."

"Oh, I'm glad."

CHANGING THE CONVERSATION: FINDING EMPATHY

You may wonder what's left to say after sidestepping all of those minefields. A lot.

Here are some things that you *can* do to get more empathically connected:

1. *Don't ask, share.* Instead of asking your teen about their thoughts and feelings, share yours instead. When adopted teens are questioned, they can feel intruded upon, pressured and examined. For example, instead of asking them if they're thinking about their birth parent on their birthday, you could instead say that *you* think about their birth parent on their birthday. This cultivates a different kind of atmosphere, an open invitation to talk.

   Luke, adopted 11th grader, had a close friend who was seriously injured in a car accident while driving under the influence. A month later, Luke's mom felt that Luke still seemed upset but wasn't sure how to broach the subject.

   I suggested that she say to Luke, "I'm still upset about what happened with Cory. I just keep thinking about it," which she did.

   Luke said, "How could he not care about himself enough to make safe decisions?" His mom was surprised, understandably so. After all, Luke had barely said two words to her for the past six months.

2. *Allow them to save face.* Sometimes teens will downplay or minimize a serious problem in order to save face. They can

feel embarrassed or even humiliated to feel so vulnerable and to feel "mothered" just intensifies those feelings. For example, it might be clear to you that they're devastated that their girlfriend broke up with them or that their best friend badmouthed them, but if they tell you that it's not a big deal, that may be why. Best to leave room for that.

3. *Stay within emotional range.* It's helpful if possible to stay within range of your adopted teen's emotions and level of intensity. That means that if your teen is upset, you should be somewhat upset. If your teen is anxious, then don't be too calm, cool and collected. If your young teen comes home upset that her crush doesn't feel the same way, it's better to say, "Oh no! I'm so sorry! That's so sad," as opposed to "Sweetie, there are plenty of fish in the sea."

Sometimes when adopted teens tell their parents about a particular struggle or disappointment, the parent ends up panicking while the teen is nonchalant about it. The opposite can also happen where the teen is beside themselves and the parent ends up a little bit too calm and put together. Staying within emotional range can help to thwart those polarizing tendencies.

For example, Rhonda, adopted tenth grader, told her mom, Beth, that she failed her math test. Her mom said, "You're kidding!"

Rhonda replied, "Nope!"

"How could you let this happen?! I thought you were doing better this quarter!"

"Mom, it's really not a big thing. Why do you always have to freak out about everything? It's just one test."

If Beth were able to stay more in emotional range, it might have gone more like this:

Rhonda: "Failed my math test."

Beth: "Really? That's surprising. Were you expecting that?"

Rhonda: "Not exactly. I sort of studied, but I didn't think I would fail."

Beth: "You're probably a little disappointed."

Rhonda: "Not really. Well, a little, I guess."

Beth: "What do you need to do to get your grade back up? You know you need to pass to stay on the swim team."

Rhonda: "She said that I could do extra credit if I show that I'm making an effort."

Beth: "So, you'll start working on that tonight?"

Rhonda: "Yeah."

4. *Speak thoughtfully about their peers.* When you speak judgmentally or critically about your adopted teens' peers, your teen may take it to heart. They're not just taking it personally because they care about their friend. They're taking it personally because they worry that the way that you feel about their peers is also the way that you feel about them. They're not always aware of it, but it's true. It's important to speak about their peers in the same nonjudgmental way that you'd talk with your teen. When you say, "Well, Donna isn't taking her life seriously and she'll never make it with that attitude," it hurts your teen's feelings.

5. *Give them some time.* These things take time. When you're in the throes of these emotional conversations, there is often a sense of urgency. Many adopted teens talk with me about feeling guilty that they're not getting better

fast enough. Although it's important to be engaged and involved, it's also important to clearly convey that they'll have the time they need to work through their struggles. You'll be there for them no matter how long it takes. There is no time limit. You're not running out of time. They can take the time that they need.

6. *Lead with understanding.* When we convey understanding, we are saying that we know where they're coming from. That should come before reassurance. For example, your teen could say something like, "Why don't you just leave me behind? Everyone else does." Although you might be inclined to say something like, "I would never do that because I'm your parent and that's never going to change," it would be more comforting for the teen if you were to say, "You've been through a lot already and I can understand why you would want to prepare yourself for the worst."

REMEMBER...

It takes courage for adopted teens to lead their complicated lives. The stakes feel high to them too. When they feel undesirable, or betrayed or disappointed, it takes courage to get back in there, even when they don't want to, even when they're scared.

It takes courage for you to parent them, too. So much feels emotionally loaded that it can be overwhelming, at times. You don't have to completely overhaul who you are as a parent. Just find a place to start that feels comfortable for you, and go from there. It's best to work on one deliberate step at a time, like asking fewer questions or leading with understanding. As you integrate each step you can add another.

Chapter 6
Envisioning the Future

For many adopted teens, facing young adulthood is like traveling alone in a place they've never been, in the dark of night, with no compass or flashlight. They cannot envision their future—what it could look like or who they could be in it, which can be terrifying. But in order to forge a path into adulthood that is unique to them, they will need to work through old hurts, fears and questions about their birth parents and their adoptive parents. The path is up to them, but you can bring the flashlight, compass and maybe some kind of map!

Adopted teens can't do their part though until they wrestle with their identity. In order to do that, they need to have wrestled with who they are now so that they can begin to envision who they could be later. Who am I? Who do I want to be? Where am I from? Where am I going? How do I identify myself? What does my race mean to me? How about my gender or age? Who am I as a daughter or son, student and adoptee? Trying to make sense of their identity can be like seeing themselves in a badly cracked mirror with several pieces missing. Their reflection is disjointed and incohesive.

FALLING SHORT

Rachel, adopted from Romania at 16 months, now 20 years old, described herself as feeling lost when she started seeing me for therapy. A college sophomore, she was majoring in economics.

Her adoptive parents, Ben and Michelle, both worked at a bank in high-level positions. They first met in business school and were married two years later.

When I asked her how school was going, she just shrugged her shoulders.

"Fine, I guess."

"How has economics been?"

Rachel slumped on the couch in my office. "Fine."

"You don't seem that excited about it," I said.

"I don't have any problems with it," she said flatly.

"Aren't your parents in banking?" I asked.

"Yeah, but they went to Harvard Business School, so kind of different, if you know what I mean."

"You mean that they didn't struggle in school like you did. School came more easily to them."

Rachel snorted. "Yeah. I just wish someone in my family knew how to draw. "

"Like you do. I remember your sketches. They were amazing!"

"I mean, they try to be interested and supportive and whatnot, but anyway."

Rachel rolled her eyes in frustration.

We both sat back.

"But it doesn't feel like enough," I said.

Rachel nodded.

"Could you ever picture yourself working in a bank?"

Rachel furrowed her eyebrows, picked up her phone then put it down again. "Probably not."

"Hmm. But you majored in it…"

"I honestly don't know what I was thinking. It just seemed like a good idea at the time."

Rachel looked dazed, almost as if she had emotionally checked out.

How did Rachel end up majoring in a subject that she wasn't that interested in?

A few possible reasons:

Rachel was inspired by her parents' success and had hoped to follow in their footsteps. Unfortunately, their path didn't really match her strengths or style. In order to eventually find her way, Rachel struggled with feelings of inadequacy in not feeling like she measured up. Rachel became increasingly disillusioned before eventually finding her way as an artist.

Many adopted teens I've worked with and known feel like they don't measure up to their adoptive parents in one way or another. Sometimes it's about school or career. Other times it's about assertiveness or even their ability to express themselves. It may explain in part why adopted teens might scoff and outright reject your well-intended suggestions or ideas about what they could do with their lives. When they tell you what they're not good at, what may remain unspoken is "compared to you." It's not that you are good at everything. But you are their parent. Your future path is visible and established, making it, in their minds, the better bet than theirs, which may be invisible to them.

The same goes for appearance. Teens utilize their biological parents as points of reference when it comes to their future. As adults, they will likely resemble one or both parents when they get older. The biological parent makes it easier for the teen to envision themselves in the future, which is reassurance that they, indeed, have a future.

Many adopted teens face being the first or the only one to be a certain way in their adoptive family. They may be the first to be depressed or anxious, to have allergies or learning disabilities. It's not easy to be the first. Biological families are able to anticipate some of the emotional issues that might run in their family, such as depression, substance abuse or ADHD. This gives biological parents a running start. Adoptive parents are in a position to discover things as they come up, which can be gratifying, but also exhausting.

At times, when adopted teens feel immobilized about their future, it's because they're caught between the identities of their birth parents and their adoptive parents. For example, Rachel initially chose economics over art. She felt pulled between her adoptive parents, the bankers and her birth parents, possible artists. Who was she? Was Rachel the banker reflecting how she was raised, or the artist, reflecting where she came from? Her anguish was not about choosing her parents. It was about her identity. For her, it felt like there wasn't room for both. Because of that Rachel felt disillusioned without realizing why.

BIRTH PARENTS

I met Michelle when she was 14 years old. Michelle's biological mother was a drug addict who had been in and out of rehab for as long as Michelle could remember. Michelle's aunt stepped in when the Department of Social Services pulled Michelle out of the abusive situation when she was eight years old. Michelle still had a relationship with her mother, but seemingly on her mother's terms. At one point when Michelle was 11 years old, her mother disappeared for several months.

Michelle came in to see me when I worked at Children's Hospital, in the outpatient therapy department. She had been struggling academically in school for a while. Her guidance counselor thought that she might be depressed and suggested outside counseling.

In therapy, Michelle talked a lot about her aspiration to make better decisions than her mom had.

"I'm not going to make the same mistakes that she did," she said. "I want a better life."

But underneath her staunch pledge Michelle was scared of the unknown. What if she couldn't do it? Michelle was scared that the writing was on the wall. Was it fate? Was she just destined to follow in her mother's footsteps?

However, she was also scared of the opposite result. What if she could really stay away from drugs and stay in school and be happy? That too is a loss, though more disguised. It can be painful to surpass one's parents. Michelle would feel more separate from her mother than ever. There is much anguish in separating when you feel like you have to do that to survive. Michelle may feel guilty that she couldn't take her mother with her somehow, that she was abandoning her, even though it was actually the other way around. Michelle has every right in the world to be happy, but it can be lonely, too.

The search

Matthew had been coming in to see me since he was in fourth grade. He was adopted from Korea at six months old. Now he was 16 years old. He was a great kid, one who had often thought about his birth parents through the years. He was also creative, funny and thoughtful. But Matthew had a lot on his plate. He had Type I diabetes and struggled in school.

When he was younger, he dreamed that he was sent away to an orphanage after he failed his math test.

During one of our sessions Matthew said that he'd been contemplating the idea of a search. He said that he'd been thinking about it off and on for a while, but especially since his sixteenth birthday a few weeks ago. He also wondered whether he could get more medical history that way. We talked about it for a while, not just to make a decision, but to explore his feelings around it. Even the *decision* whether or not to search is a way to exploring their identity. For some, it's simple, but for others, it's an ongoing decision that they revisit over time.

Later that evening, I got a concerned voice-mail from Matthew's mom, Lisa.

"I just had an interesting conversation with Matthew. Apparently you told him that this would be a good time to search for his birth parents. I wish you had discussed this with me first. This is something that I would have liked to talk with him about first. Can you give me a call?"

Lisa believed that the topic of searching should be introduced in a certain way at a certain time, similar to the "sex" talk or being a safe driver. But the search is not a new topic. It's embedded in the adoption experience. For Matthew, this wasn't about Lisa. This was about his missing information that he felt that he needed in order to develop his identity. When adoptees initiate a search for their birth parents they are also searching for their own identity, any insights or answers that might help them do that.

For adopted teens, the idea of searching for one's birth parents is intriguing. On one hand, why wouldn't they want to know everything they can about the person who gave birth to them? On the other hand, to search would mean returning to a time when they had no voice, no control and no power. Whatever they decide, it's complicated. If they choose not to search they might be missing out on pertinent life information but if they do they risk feeling rejected and abandoned again.

WHEN ABANDONMENT ISSUES AND IDENTITY ISSUES COLLIDE

Jeff was a 19-year-old Vietnamese adoptee who came to see me because he was confused about his path in life. He had taken a year after high school to work and was considering going to college but had no idea what he wanted to study, or even whether he even wanted to go at all. He felt immobilized.

Jeff described himself as the easy one in the family growing up, someone who never got angry or fell apart. His older brother Nick continued to struggle with depression and substance abuse. But as Jeff reflected on his high school years he knew something was off.

"I had a lot of friends. I played in a band. No one ever gave me a hard time about being Asian. It really didn't come up at all."

"The whole four years, it never came up?" I asked. "That's kind of striking, isn't it?"

"Yeah, I guess." Jeff looked off into space, dazed.

"Would you say that you were happy then?"

"That's what I wanted everyone to believe. And, sometimes I did too. But no, I think it was more like, if everyone liked me then I was happy."

"But you're saying that you aren't sure you really were happy most of the time," I remarked. "You wanted to be liked but even when you did successfully achieve that, I think there might be a moment of relief, but not happiness. And then you just do it all over again. It never ends."

He sighed. "Yeah. Looking back I think I was numb. I didn't even know what I was doing."

"Why is it so important to make the *right* decision? What does that mean to you?" I said.

Jeff sat quietly, still pondering.

Then he looked at me. "When I realized what had happened, that I had been adopted and my birth mother had abandoned me, I vowed that I would show her that she made a mistake."

"A mistake?"

"That she never should have given me up."

"How would you *show* her that?"

"By being really successful."

"So you feel like you have something to prove to her?"

"Yes."

Jeff had colliding agendas. He wanted to avoid rejection and abandonment, prove to his birth mother that she made a mistake in giving him up and figure out what he wanted to do with his life. His best chance at being happy and fulfilled is to better understand his fears of loss and abandonment and work through his feelings of helplessness about his birth mother giving him up. This will free him up to come into his own and lead a life that is true to who he is.

WHEN EMOTIONS RUN HIGH

Kathleen had just graduated from high school. She had come a long way. She had stopped drinking and smoking and her grades had also improved. Her parents agreed to supplement her rent while she attended community college and worked part-time. She was planning to move in with a few friends to keep costs down.

But in my family session with Kathleen and her father Joe, Joe didn't hold back.

His shoulders tensed, he said, "Kathleen, you know that all of the other bills—cable, Internet, the car payments, phone, all of that is up to you. We agreed to cover your rent up to a certain amount, but that is as far as we're willing to go. And, by the way, if you get into trouble with those bills, we're not prepared to bail you out. It's your responsibility to make sure that you don't end up in debt."

It wasn't as much what her father said as it was how he said it. Joe was emphatic and almost seemed angry.

Kathleen got quieter, saying, "I know, I know."

I leaned in slightly.

"So, Joe, the plan is important and I agree that it's good to be detailed and specific. But from what you're saying, adulthood just really seems like a bad idea. Why would anyone want to grow up if they're just headed into that mess?"

Her father took a deep breath.

"Okay. I might have gotten a little carried away."

"The way that you're talking about it and your tone almost makes it seem like you expect her to fail. But she hasn't. We're just getting started with it!"

"I know how much Kathleen wants this," Joe said, turning to her. "You've been working hard, I recognize that. But I want you to be prepared."

There's plenty to worry about. And, as an adoptive parent you have the added challenge of questioning, "Is this genetic?" It's a lifetime wildcard, which may further deepen your anxiety about what's around the bend for them.

WORDS

Your adopted teen needs you to be optimistic about their life, open to what the future might hold, accepting of where they are in this journey and realistic when necessary.

When you say things such as:

1. *"If you can't even make it through two tests without falling apart, you'll never make it in college!"* your teen may hear, "You're a failure, you're behind where you should be and I'll probably continue to be disappointed for a long time."

   Alternative—"If you definitely want to go to college in the fall, we really need to figure out some better ways to manage the homework. That way you'll feel more ready when the time comes."

2. *"How can you just throw your life away when you smoke and drink?"* Your teen may hear, "I have no idea what to do with you. I never made the mistakes that you're making right now."

   Alternative—"You make certain decisions regarding drugs and alcohol, which I'm sure I don't totally understand. It may limit certain opportunities, which you know. I've also seen that you are capable of being responsible at times, and I appreciate that."

3. *"If you get into trouble with those bills, we're not prepared to bail you out." "It's your responsibility to make sure that you don't end up in debt,"* as Joe had said. Your teen may hear, "I know this is going to blow up in my face. You're going to screw this up somehow and I'm going to have to pick up the pieces."

   Alternative—"I think the plan is pretty straightforward. That's great! I'm glad we came to some decisions.

Things will probably come up, and when they do, we'll try to figure them out as we go along."

STRENGTHS AND STYLE

Lucy, freshman in high school, told me that she never thought about the future.

"I never think about things before they happen," she said, when I asked her how she might want to spend her summer.

In our parent meeting, her mom Miranda lamented, "I don't know what else to do. I keep asking, 'Have you come up with a summer plan yet? The deadlines are coming up. If you wait too long everything'll be filled up.'"

I told Miranda that I could try to talk with Lucy about it during our next session.

This was how it went.

"Have you thought much about what you might want to do this summer?"

"No, not really."

"So, last year you went to that swim camp…what did you think of that?"

"Okay, fine I guess."

"Would you want to do that again?"

"Maybe, I really don't know."

Lucy looked dazed.

"If you could do anything you wanted this summer what would you want to do? Sports, get a job, travel…"

She perked up a little bit. "Travel? I like to travel."

"Are you serious?"

I'll admit that I was a little surprised.

"That's true. You're athletic and you love outdoor stuff, right?"

She nodded.

Well, she ended up in Alaska that summer doing wildlife conservation and after became interested in rehabilitating animals who have been mistreated and malnourished.

A few things to note about this conversation:

1. *Not about adoption.* It was not about her birth parents or her adoptive parents. It was about just her. For adopted teens, your best chance at helping them to develop their future identity is through utilizing their strengths and their style. By strengths, of course, I mean what they're good at, their talents and abilities that are specific to them. By style, I mean their way of being in the world. You can help them more with discovering their strengths and style than you can with working through some of the adoption issues that they wrestle with.

2. *Saying it out loud.* It can be useful to provide that input for adopted teens when it comes to their future. With teens, I've said things like, "So, you're not someone who will be happy in a cubicle. You need variety, maybe a little bit of danger, is that right?" Or, I might say, "You have such an eye. I could see you being a buyer for a clothing store where you travel all over the world." I often add, "Could you ever picture yourself doing something like that?" I want them to actively think about it, not just hear me. Remember, they're walking towards the future in the dark. Even if I'm off base, they become intrigued with the idea of discovering more about who they are and who they could become. But when you get it right, the teen can feel seen and understood.

3. *Prioritize real-life, real-time experiences.* I had just had my second interview for a job at a residential treatment facility. My first interview with the director seemed promising, but the second one was with Dana who

would be my supervisor. For some reason, she just really did not like me. I have no idea why, to this day. But whatever the reason, this was unsettling.

I just thought to myself, if she's this angry with me already and I haven't even started, that doesn't bode well. Would I just be setting myself up for failure? I was offered the job. I didn't know what to do so I called my mother and explained what had happened.

She listened carefully. Then she surprised me.

"I think you should do it," she said emphatically.

"Really? You're kidding!"

"No, I'm not kidding." Mom then turned on her life lessons voice that I've been privy to countless times. "Katie, you're going to have to work with all kinds of people in your life. They're not all going to like you! I think this a really important experience for you to have. If this job is the kind of experience you need and you're qualified for it, you should do it."

So, I did. I took the job for the experience. Dana hated me the entire year and a half I worked there, first as a youth care worker than as a theater teacher. It wasn't easy. But what an opportunity. I'm a better clinician because of it, that's for sure.

It wasn't just my mother's advice that finalized my decision. It was her belief that the best learning comes from challenging yourself.

4. *Take the lead.* Bruce, father of Sam, adopted 17-year-old, expressed concern that his son wasn't showing enough interest in his future in his parent guidance meeting.

"He never brings up college at all," Bruce lamented. "He's doing pretty well in school. I think it would be a good idea to go around and look at a few schools for April vacation but I don't think he'd agree to it."

"Have you asked him?"

"No, I don't know if I'm going to."

"Why?"

"What if he says no? Do I force him?"

I said, "Just tell him that that you'd like to take him to see some schools over April vacation. He can always refuse, but I don't think he will. Don't ask him. Just let him know that that would be a good next step."

The father seemed doubtful but said that he would do that.

The following week I saw Sam, his son, for his therapy appointment.

"So, are you going to be around for April vacation week?" I asked.

"Actually, no. My dad wants to take a trip to see some colleges around the area, so we'll be gone the whole week."

"Oh, okay. That seems good. Looking forward to it?"

Sam nodded.

Whether it's college trips or summer plans, they do look to you to set the expectations. They need job experience, and not just their generous neighbor's job: a real job that they apply for with a paycheck and the risk of being fired. If your teen isn't quite ready to get a job that helps to cultivate their interests, volunteering is a great option. They should be doing something in the community. Their best chance at developing their identity in the world is to be out experiencing the world.

5. *When it's better for them to say no.* Charlotte was a Chinese adoptee and a sophomore in high school. Her mother Jean got in touch with me because Charlotte seemed to be increasingly withdrawn and tearful, possibly depressed.

"She's such a perfectionist," her mom told me in our first parent meeting. "I hate to see her being so hard on herself." As I got to know the family, I found out that Charlotte's schedule was packed. She did debate, dance, cello, field hockey and even took meals to the elderly on weekends.

When I asked her mother if it was possible that Charlotte was overbooked, Jean replied, "Well, she's so good at just about everything she does!"

In her individual session I asked Charlotte about her schedule.

She said, "I don't even like half the stuff I do anymore."

"But there are certain things that you still love to do?"

She smiled. "Yes, I love dance. If I could do that all the time, I would."

"And cello?"

"Well, just so-so."

Charlotte was out and about, she was impressive, but she wasn't happy. There were certain things in her schedule that seemed to have accumulated over the years that she had really outgrown, like debate team and the cello.

Ideally, you want your adopted teen's life to reflect who they are, not just who they believe that they should be. When we streamlined Charlotte's life a little bit, she felt more like herself.

6. *Embrace differences.* I remember talking with Becca, 17-year-old Guatemalan adoptee, about her "style." It began with us talking about what kind of job she might get for the summer and then what she might want to do with her life after school. Becca said that she enjoyed being outside and liked jobs that weren't wildly variable

but fairly consistent from day to day. She wasn't someone who loved having people pepper her with questions or demands, so retail wasn't ideal. And she didn't want to sit around all day. "So, you're saying that you don't want to be…a therapist, is that what you're saying?" I said, laughing, pretending to be hurt.

Becca laughed too. "No, not really. Anyway, I would go crazy if I had to listen to people go whine about their problems for hours. Do you seriously like that?"

I thought for a second. "I do love it, but I can see why it wouldn't be for everyone."

One way to help is to notice differences in style between you and your teen. Style is not evaluative; no one is better or worse, just different. Sometimes teens learn more from differences than they do from similarities. When I joked with Becca about her not wanting to be a therapist, I wanted Becca to know that differences will not threaten our relationship, only enrich it. The ways in which we're different are just as important and in some ways, even more important because they're often less articulated.

Because adopted teens can't or don't necessarily want to do the same thing that their adoptive parents do, they need their parents' help to discover and highlight those skills and strengths that aren't mentioned. It's not a compliment that they need. It's information. For example, you could say, "Hmm. You've really done well saving your money over the years. You keep track of it. You always know how much you have. That could be useful to you someday, in your own budgeting, but also even as a job working with money. Do you think that might ever be something that you would be interested in?"

REMEMBER...

For adopted teens, envisioning their future, developing their identity, both current and future, doesn't just happen. That process is complicated and emotional. But where you can be most helpful is in developing and clarifying their strength and style. This is the flashlight and the compass that they need. With your help, it might not be quite as dark and they may not feel quite as lost.

This is the fourth parenting task. You've come a long way.

Chapter 7

Privilege, Race and Cultural Norms

Making It Personal

Although this chapter refers to the experience of parenting Asian transracial adoptees, my hope is that, even if you're outside of that demographic, in some ways, the themes that I explore are universal. Stereotypes, assumptions, safety, privilege and identity are part of all of our lives in one way or another.

Many Asian adoptees are born into one race and culture and raised in another. This experience offers unique complications for Asian adoptees in feeling loved and empowered. It can impact their sense of belonging and identity. Asian adopted teens are a minority within a minority group. Asian adoptees often feel different from white people because they're not white and they differ culturally from other Asians. Without the perfect fit, they are vulnerable to the perceptions and viewpoints of others.

I discuss:

- a different take on privilege, white or otherwise

- racial and cultural norms versus stereotypes

- experiences with Asians from Asian families
- differences between the Black and the Asian experience
- a new way to talk about racism
- why it's so important to manage your outrage.

Cathy, 14, had been taught to be proud of being a Chinese adoptee. She felt prepared for any racial slur that came her way. She had done the "anti-bullying" workshops and still had the books to prove it. Her family did everything possible to ensure that she felt empowered and confident. Cathy's parents were involved in Families with Children from China (FCC), and still kept in touch with other children from her orphanage. Her circle of friends at school was a mix of Asian and white.

One day, her Chinese nonadopted friends were making plans to go to a special Chinese New Year celebration. They were talking about it before biology class.

Cathy, assuming that she was invited, said, "Sounds fun! What time?"

Janie, one of the girls looked over at her, surprised. "Oh, sorry, we figured that you wouldn't want to because, you know, you're not really that Chinese."

Cathy felt humiliated. She got up and walked out of the classroom. Cathy tried to pull herself together but just ended up sobbing in the bathroom for 25 minutes before she left school and walked home.

Later that evening, her mother Lydia tried to talk with her about what had happened.

"Sweetie," she said. "Listen, I really think they weren't trying to leave you out or hurt your feelings. They're your friends!"

"I know Mom, but don't you see! It was so embarrassing! How could I be so stupid?"

Her mom said, "I'm sure that they'd love to have you join them. If you just asked…" Before her mom could finish her thought, Cathy stalked up to her room and shut the door.

VULNERABILITY

The situation with her friends triggered Cathy's deepest fears of being rejected and alone. In that moment, she felt abandoned by her friends and misunderstood by her mother. She was also disappointed that she couldn't just take it in stride. Cathy thought that she had "trained" well. She wondered, how could I have not seen this coming? And why didn't I know what to say? All of those books, workshops, groups and culture camps felt like a waste of time. Cathy was also confused. Had her friend suggested that she wasn't Chinese? Once and for all, was she Chinese or not? But the situation brought to the surface feelings that had, until then, flown under the radar. It was just a matter of time. Her parents' message, "Be proud of who you are and never let anyone tell you any different," emphasized strength but didn't acknowledge vulnerability.

MY TAKE ON "PRIVILEGE"

The issue of who does and doesn't have "*privilege*" can become quickly contentious. For white adoptive parents with nonwhite children it's especially charged. While some parents resonate with the idea, others resent the assertion that they are privileged, saying that they've never been privileged a day in their life. Some parents resent the implication that they've been pampered or indulged and feel pressured to feel guilty for something that they didn't do.

Peggy McIntosh, author of "White privilege: unpacking the invisible white knapsack,"[1] defines white privilege this way:

> Privilege exists when one group has something of value that is denied to others simply because of the groups they belong to, rather than because of anything they've done or failed to do. Access to privilege doesn't determine one's outcomes, but it is definitely an asset that makes it more likely that whatever talent, ability, and aspirations a peson with privilege has will result in something positive for them.

Peggy compiled a list of ways that she could see white privilege play out in her everyday life, including:

> 1. I can, if I wish, arrange to be in the company of people of my race most of the time.

> 10. Whether I use checks, credit cards, or cash, I can count on my skin color not to work against the appearance of financial reliability.

> 15. I am never asked to speak for all the people of my racial group.

The concept of privilege is not only about race.

I define my privilege as a benefit that I can take for granted, that I didn't earn. When I go to a building, I don't worry about it being handicapped accessible. When I talk

---

1   McIntosh, P. (1990) "White privilege: unpacking the invisible knapsack." *Independent School 49*, 2, 31–5. Accessed on 06/01/2017 at www. ywcamadison.org/atf/cf/%7B2487BD0F-90C7-49BC-858D-CC50637ECE23%7D/RJClass_White_Privilege_unpacking_knapsack.pdf

about my husband at work, I don't worry about hostility regarding my sexual orientation because I'm straight.

Background: Chicago

Privilege is not all about race.

I grew up in Hyde Park, former President Obama's neighborhood, on the South Side of Chicago. The student body of my public high school was 84 percent Black. My school often had police cars stationed out front, mainly to head off trouble. Sophomore year, my friend Tamara (white) and I were headed off-campus for lunch and a police officer asked us to get into the car. We answered a bunch of questions about where we were going and why. That went on for about 15 minutes. And, although it was a first, I was not concerned about my safety. In fact, I was confident, cocky about the whole thing.

Later, in band class, I was chatting with my friend John, African-American, tall, dark and lanky. He walked in slow motion and was the opposite of aggressive. He wasn't extroverted but not hard to get to know either if you tried. I played flute; he played saxophone.

I was low-key but still held that sureness. "So, the police stopped Tamara and me in fifth period and they ended up, like, questioning us in the car for like 20 minutes."

John responded in his understated friendly way with his low voice, "Oh, really. Man, that sucks."

"Have they ever done that to you?"

"Oh, yeah."

"Really? What happened?"

"They pushed me up against the car and said, 'Are you carrying any weapons?' I said, 'No, sir. I'm not.' They said, 'I hope you're not lying to me.'"

I knew that this happens too much, and that this story may seem mild in light of today's level of violence, particularly with police officers and members of the Black community. Remember, I was 15 years old and this was before the Internet. It got personal for me in a way that it previously hadn't.

Neither John nor I had done anything wrong. But John was assumed guilty until proven otherwise. My presumed innocence was a benefit that I hadn't earned and his presumed guilt was a status that he didn't deserve.

In this situation, I was the privileged one. You may be thinking, that's not privilege, that's just basic common decency. That's true. But because racial equality isn't adhered to, it becomes a privilege, not a right.

What about you? Can you think of a time when you were on one side or the other?

Before graduate school, I worked in a summer program for children and teens with emotional and/or behavioral issues. I worked with ten-year-old boys. Four out of ten kids in our group were Black; six were white. There were five staff along with our supervisor; everyone else besides me was white.

We had a Visitors Day when parents, families and caretakers came to visit the kids. To prepare, we went the extra mile to make clear to each family that their kids were well taken care of. The kids were showered and squeaky clean for the big day and we spent hours laundering *all* of their clothes. Just as the visitors began to arrive, a staff member, Black, from another group took one look at Jerome, one of our kids, and said, "Come with me, I need to fix your hair," which he did.

We had missed it. Jerome's hair was a mess. In some ways, it was an honest mistake. We were busy and didn't know. But the situation reflected the challenge of being a minority with needs that are often missed. As an isolated incident, one could argue that there was no harm done. But for those outside of the majority, these kinds of things happen more than you realize. Over time this can erode morale and lead minorities to feel unseen, unattended to and misunderstood.

Many years ago, I did a presentation to a group of experienced medical staff at a hospital in Boston about clinical work with transracially-adopted children. In the midst of my presentation, one of the psychologists on staff raised her hand. She was African-American, one of two in the room in a sea of white people, and me.

She said, "You're doing a lot of talking about Asian and Black adoptees. I think you're minimizing the impact and the experience of being Black. Are you suggesting that the Asian experience and the Black experience are comparable? Because, to me, there is no comparison."

I paused then said, "I think you're right. If I had to choose, yes, I would say that it's harder to be Black than it is to be Asian."

To this day, I'm not sure whether she was referring to the Black experience, or Black kids who are adopted into white families, but regardless, I respected her for raising the issue.

When it comes to the stereotypes associated with Asians and those associated with African-Americans, there's fairly little overlap, and the effect is often indirect and unprovable. When I worked in community mental health, some of us who work with children were chatting about race, life and clinical work. In my private practice, those who come in to see me for psychotherapy already know me as a Korean-adoptee. But at the clinic, families were assigned to us. One of my colleagues, Trisha, who was Black, happened to mention that in first meetings with parents, the parent will often advise her on the best ways to connect with their child. Peter, also Black, said that the same thing happens to him. I found that interesting because my experience was very different. In fact,

I couldn't recall a time when a parent advised me on how to handle their child. Trisha and Peter had more years and expertise doing clinical work than I. I suggested that their race might change the way that certain families interacted with them, especially in the beginning. Was it possible that parents were unconsciously responding to the destructive societal Black stereotype of being less intelligent? It's possible.

I could have attributed the difference to me, that perhaps I just exuded so much clinical authority and ability that no one would ever think to advise me. But I don't think that was it. This was a privilege that I didn't earn.

ASIAN CULTURE OR STEREOTYPE?

Years ago, I facilitated a workshop for ten nine-year-old Asian adopted children. This weekend retreat was held especially for Asian adoptive families. Asian college students were the camp counselors, which everyone loved, especially the kids. They also assisted in my groups.

I met with the kids twice over the weekend and then with the parents. Our first group meeting focused mainly on adoption issues and our second on Asian stereotypes.

I wanted the children to experience stereotypes in a nondamaging but personal way. I created a list of Asian stereotypes and wrote each stereotype on a separate notecard.

These stereotypes/assumptions included:

- doesn't speak English

- plays violin

- foreigner

- math whiz

- quiet

- strict Asian parents
- excels in school.

Then I affixed one notecard to each child's back. One by one, they would try to guess their stereotype based on how the others interacted with them.

For example, with the boy who "couldn't speak English" the others spoke extra loudly and slowly. When it was time for him to guess his stereotype, he said, "Am I stupid?"

For the girl who was "quiet," the others would say things like, "Oh, are you going to the party tonight? Oh, probably not, right?"

Or, with the foreigner stereotype, they would say, "Do your parents speak English?" or "Is this a whole new world for you?"

The kids loved it. Whenever one would finish, the others would say, "My turn, my turn!"

But try to imagine this experience in real life. Like Peter and Trisha, there's something off but you can't put your finger on what it is. How does one make sense of that? To be on the receiving end of stereotypes and assumptions isn't straightforward. So often, people are unaware of their own deeply held prejudices and/or cultural generalizations.

After we finished the stereotype exercise, all of us sat around in a circle of chairs.

I asked, "Are all Asians quiet?"

They looked at one another and vigorously shook their heads.

"No!"

"Are all Asians good at math?"

"No!"

Do all Asians have strict parents?"

They'd yell, "No!"

We were really getting into it.

Then, the college student, Nancy, who was sitting next to me, said, quietly, "Those things are kind of true. My parents are really strict. They always put our schoolwork ahead of everything else. And they speak mostly Korean at home."

Then she added, "Oh, and I don't play violin but I do play cello."

There is a fine line between a stereotype and a cultural norm. We were advocating for individuality, wanting to feel empowered, not oppressed. But I wondered how Nancy had heard it. Did it seem like were proud of how "un-Asian" we were? Had we embodied the "American" stereotype of being self-involved, entitled and oblivious? Maybe so.

Logically, I knew that Asian adoptees do not exist in a vacuum. We are in the context of nonadopted Asian and white nonadoptive families. But, in that moment, it really hit home. I shifted our conversation to what it's like to figure out what you're *not* first before you can figure out who you are. Then we talked about the ways that they do line up with Asian stereotypes or cultural generalizations.

One said, smiling sheepishly, "Well, I do get good grades."

Another gestured to a girl sitting across from him, "You are kind of quiet!"

Everyone giggled.

Stereotypes are automatic, exaggerated, judgmental views regarding a particular race and/or culture. Stereotypes are not open to individual differences or new information. They are often based on little to no information or exposure, and stated in a way that discourages conversation or exploration.

Example—"Asian parents are obsessed with school. They don't even let their kids have a life."

Racial and cultural norms are beliefs and actions that illustrate the personality of a culture. Shared expectations and rules, both spoken and unspoken, are a part of cultural norms. They are based on relevant information, experience and individual differences. Beliefs about racial and cultural norms are humble, not judgmental or critical.

Example—"Asian parents do not take academic success for granted. My experience has been that school tends to take higher priority over social relationships and playing sports."

Cultural norms are humble and *porous*. Stereotypes are impenetrable.

I've had my own personal experiences with Asian cultural norms. It is based on the many Asian families I've known throughout the years, although far fewer compared to the number of white families I've known.

Ben Kim was my Korean violinist friend whom I knew through my teen years. We played in the same orchestra. I played flute. Ben told me that his mother would take notes during his violin lesson and repeat her notes out loud to him when he'd practice at home. When it came time to apply to college, Ben applied to 17. I applied to two. We were both Korean but Ben's family was also Korean, unlike mine, of course.

Did our cultural difference reflect Asian culture?

When I asked Ben what he thought, he said, "Oh, yeah, this is the Korean way, you always have to be at the top, achievement-wise."

I did a consultation for parents in a nonadopted Chinese family whose seven-year-old son Liam was having several meltdowns a week. Deborah, Liam's mom, used the example of what would happen when it was time for his piano lesson.

"He'll just refuse to come to the piano," Deborah lamented. "He'll sit sulking on the stairs. It's embarrassing for me, incredibly rude to the teacher. What do I do?"

"Well," I said, "just so I know, how essential is it that he take piano?"

She said, her tone intensifying, "Oh, he's not quitting piano. That's not an option. I'm *that* Chinese mom that's like, 'You're so doing this.'"

Given that many Asian adoptees are more culturally American than not, it can be confusing to have others attribute Asian stereotypes and cultural norms to them. Asian adoptees are so often trying to figure out who they're not, before they can figure out who they are.

Math was never my thing. My sophomore year in high school, I was at risk of failing geometry. At one point, we were standing around our teacher's desk and I asked him when we'd get our tests back. He said that he would pass them out at the end of the period.

I said, "Well, can you just tell me if I passed?"

A kid in my class, Black, standing next to me muttered, "Yeah, right," as he went to sit down.

It threw me.

Did he think that I was one of those A students who always say that they failed? Did he assume that because I was Asian? Or, did he have other reasons for believing me to be a good student? We'll never know for sure.

But whatever the reason, he was mistaken.

THE ASIAN-ADOPTEE EXPERIENCE

"Where are you from?"

I've literally been asked this question hundreds of times. It's difficult in that it's intrusive and personal.

Where *are* we from? There are so many questions in this question. Where were we born? Where did we grow up? Who are we racially? Culturally? It's a hard question to answer even if we wanted to.

Many of us have tried to sidestep it by saying, "Boston," or "Michigan," but know that it will not be enough. Their next question is inevitably, "No, I mean, where are you really from?" And, if that question doesn't yield the answer that they're looking for, they'll often ask, "No, I mean, where is your family from?"

We know that they want the country—Korea, China, etc. We don't want to be rude and yet it can be difficult to end the conversation without telling them what they feel entitled to know, as if it's public domain.

Beginning in teenhood, this question, "Where are you from?" can also become a popular pick-up line, putting Asians, particularly Asian women, in a tough spot. If they aren't interested in the questioner, then it's difficult to sidestep the conversation without feeling rude. And, if they keep saying, "Boston," or "Michigan," that can anger the questioner which can be uncomfortable and possibly even risky.

You might be wondering, "Why not just say 'Korea' and get it over with?" Sometimes, I do that. But I resent the pressure to feel obligated to provide information about myself to strangers who for the most part are more curious than interested. I often recommend to Asian women that they say something like, "For me, that's a personal question and I don't feel comfortable talking about personal things with strangers."

The "war" years

For many years, it wasn't uncommon for me to be randomly approached by war veterans who then said hello in Chinese, Japanese or Vietnamese. This has happened in post offices, grocery parking lots and shopping centers. When I looked bewildered, they often said something like, "Oh, I could have sworn that you were Vietnamese. I fought in the Vietnam war," as if that justified what they were doing. It did feel intrusive and inappropriate, but even more importantly it reminded me of the power of race in people's lives. They weren't interested in me. I represented something to them. All that mattered to them was that I was Asian. And, although I kept the interaction short, there was a way that I felt guilty, as if they needed my forgiveness somehow.

"I thought you were someone else"

It isn't uncommon for me to have a white male see me in a public setting like a drug store, and mistake me for someone else. To make matters worse, when they see me, they'll look sort of angry. Then, after a few seconds, when they realize that, oops, I'm not that person, they'll say something like, "Oh, I thought you were someone else." But they'll still be angry, as if my very presence has dredged up past wrongdoings. A bad breakup, perhaps? Again, I can feel the pull of their projections and it almost makes me want to play it out. I have the urge to say, "Look, it just didn't work out. Get over it!"

There are variations to this theme. When I meet someone, they often say something like, "Haven't we met before?"

I'll say, "No, I don't think so."

Sometimes they're insistent. "Are you sure? I'm trying to figure out where I've seen you before."

Then, they'll say, "Did you ever have a child at The Park School?" Or wherever.

"No."

I'm just waiting for it to play out.

You might be thinking, well, maybe they do know you! Maybe, but it's happened so much. In addition, if they did know me, there's a good chance that I would also know them. I don't forget a face that easily.

Why would this happen? Do all Asians look alike? Yes, if you've only seen a handful of them, don't live with them and attend to the ways that each of us looks unique. We are more than just "the Asian one."

Model minority

This suggests that Asians are doing well socioeconomically, in school and generally well in society and at home—in other words, most similar to "white" values and standards. No one likes a teacher's pet. And this stereotype about the Asian community perpetuates resentment and divisiveness. It can feel shaming for Asians who don't meet that level of perfection, including kids with learning disabilities and lower-income families.

Asian fetish or yellow fever

Urban Dictionary defines this term as "usually applied to white males who have a *clear sexual preference for women of Asian descent*, although it can also be used in reference to white females who prefer Asian men" (my emphasis).[2]

Over time, many Asian women are rudely awakened to the presence of the Asian fetish. Because a lot of their dating world is online, much of the preference for Asian women comes more quickly to the surface. According to many of my Asian female clients, some don't hold back in what they think. They'll say things like, "Asian women are so hot," or "I dig Asian women, for sure."

Now, it may seem like a compliment that many men seem to prefer Asian women. But when being Asian is one of

---

2   Accessed on 06/01/17 at www.urbandictionary.com/define.php?term= yellow%20fever

your best features, one can't help but question which cultural stereotypes might also be in play. Cate Matthews (*Huffington Post*, 16 September 2014) in her article, "Here's What 'Yellow Fever' Really Means,"[3] states that "Men with 'yellow fever' look at you and they only see school girls or sexual geishas."

Asian adopted teens, particularly female, are in the middle of this, whether they realize it or not. Does that mean that there's no potential for white men to be suitable boyfriends and husbands? Absolutely not. Many Asian women are happily married to white men, myself included. In discussing this with several Asian adopted friends, one said, "My husband probably started out with yellow fever too! But now things are different." But, if they've only dated Asian women, that's a red flag.

But it's complicated. For women, the white standard of beauty could be described as thin, petite frame, soft and lovely. Obviously, this standard is ridiculous. But, even so, there are ways that the stereotype and/or cultural norm for Asian women overlap. For some men who are white, dating an Asian woman feels like less of a leap than dating a woman who is Black or Latino.

For Asian men, it's a different story. Tall, dark and handsome is the old-school white measure of attractiveness. Sometimes women joke that they will never date someone whose butt is smaller than theirs. And, although we've come a long way in blurring the gender roles, society still communicates certain measures of attractiveness for men. Big and strong, smart, authoritative, extroverted and financially successful. Many happy couples do not fit these roles, of course, but many Asian adopted men I've known and worked with are haunted by them. The Asian male stereotype is skinny, bookish or nerdy, short and not authoritative or a leader, at

3   Accessed on 06/01/17 at www.huffingtonpost.com/2014/07/29/anna-akana-asian-girls_n_5628201.html

least not according to white male standards. Another Asian male stereotype involves the small size of their genitalia. You might be thinking, surely that's not a real stereotype, and even if it is, surely Asian adopted males aren't giving it any credence. Unfortunately it is, and they are, more than you know. It intensifies their insecurities about their maleness and makes it more difficult to be confident in the dating world.

WHITE STANDARD OF BEAUTY: BEYOND THE UNITED STATES

The white standard of beauty doesn't just impact Asian adoptees. It impacts Asians everywhere. South Korea has the highest rate of surgery per capita in the world, according to some statistics. The double-eyelid surgery adds a line to Asians' eyelids. Those who are white usually have this line but about half of Asians do not.

Why is this line so necessary?

The features that make Asians look more Asian—such as the monolid, almond shaped eyes, the flatter face and the less defined nose—are not perceived as desirable or attractive compared to features associated with being white.

This issue frequently comes up in my practice with both genders. One Asian adopted male described the great pains that he took to create a Facebook profile picture that deemphasized the flatness of his face and made his eyes look bigger. Incidentally, I liked his other pictures a lot better! One girl told me that she doesn't like to part her hair because it looks too Asian. Another girl told me that she just inherently believes that white girls are prettier.

BULLYING VERSUS TEASING

There's a difference between bullying and teasing.

- *Teasing*—The intent of teasing is not to not to hurt someone's feelings. Teasing can be playful and affectionate with friends or family, but can be misplaced or unintentionally hurtful. And, if and when that happens, the person doing the teasing is motivated to stop.

- *Bullying*—According to stopbullying.gov,[4] bullying is defined as "unwanted, aggressive behavior among school aged children that involves a real or perceived power imbalance. The behavior is repeated, or has the potential to be repeated, over time." In my experience, power differences can occur in status, such as a coach and a team player, or in other ways, such as someone who is more "popular" and powerful.

Morgan, domestically adopted 15-year-old, had just joined the residential treatment facility for adolescent girls. She was a freshman in high school, referred due to academic failure and depression. Morgan was shorter than average, overweight and wore glasses.

There were two cottages with about 12–15 girls per cottage. Nicole, 17, had been there for six months, tried to run away twice and assaulted a police officer when he returned her to the facility. She was tall and athletic, with long brown hair, often pulled up in a ponytail.

I was not working that evening but Morgan filled me in.

Morgan arrived at the cottage mid morning. Things seemed fine until later that evening when Nicole and two

---

4   See www.stopbullying.gov/what-is-bullying/definition

other girls approached and cornered her. Then, Nicole took Morgan's glasses right off her face.

Morgan said, "Give me back my glasses."

Nicole dangled them above her head.

"Okay, as long as you call me Queen Nicole I'll give them back to you."

"No."

"If you don't, I'm going to break your glasses."

Morgan didn't fight back or give in. She simply waited.

A few minutes later, David, one of the staff, came in and said, sternly, "Nicole, give her back her glasses right now," which Nicole did, after which she had consequences for her behavior.

I asked Morgan, "Why did you decide not to do it, to call her Queen Nicole?"

Morgan answered simply, "I knew she would keep doing it."

TIPS, MINDSETS AND STRATEGIES

Know your stereotypes

In my opinion, being educated and informed about stereotypes, Asian and other nonwhite groups, is an essential part of growing up, like not taking candy from strangers or walking alone at night. If you wait until they come up, it's a lot more difficult for your teen to process. Then they are not only processing whatever just happened, but also trying to decipher the stereotypes at the same time. Teens should learn to take responsibility for what happens in their lives. But sometimes it really isn't about them. It's about their race. When they feel unhappy with what they look like, it's not just because they personally have low self-esteem. It is because the white standard of beauty is pervasive and powerful.

Racism just comes out of nowhere

That said, it's impossible to be completely prepared for racism. It's erratic and can come out of nowhere.

When I was in high school I played the flute and attended a music camp. It was parents' weekend. Lisa, my closest flute friend, was just getting back to the cabin. She literally seemed shaky, as if she was trembling.

I asked her what was wrong.

Lisa explained that she was catching her parents up on all of the camp drama and had told them that I had a crush on a boy, Terrence, but that it seemed like he didn't like me back.

Her mom said, "You mean the clarinet player we just met, the one who was Black?"

Lisa nodded.

"Well, sweetie, maybe he knows that you just don't do that sort of thing."

"What do you mean, that sort of thing?" Lisa asked.

She told me that she suddenly had the chills.

Her mom didn't skip a beat.

"Well, he's Black right? And, she's what, Chinese or something?"

"No, she's Korean, but anyway. So, what? Are you saying that people should only date within their own race?"

Before her mom could respond, her dad jumped in, saying cheerily, "How did we get into this whole area anyway? Let's change the subject."

Lisa hadn't seen this coming and she was devastated.

When it comes to racism and racist comments and incidents, being informed about stereotypes and what happens out there is important. But you can never really know how things will unfold, and convincing yourself otherwise is just an illusion.

Manage your outrage

When your adopted teen tells you about a racist remark or incident, you may likely feel outraged. That's understandable. But it's not black and white. Your outrage may hold specific meaning for your adopted teen. Remember that your adopted teen is in the midst of exploring and possibly experimenting with their racial identity. It's likely that at some point they will think, feel, say or believe something that might be considered racist. So when they tell you about someone who said or did something racist, they may also in some ways identify with that person. When you're outraged with the person who is "racist," they may take it personally. "If my parent can be this intolerant of that guy when he says some off color thing, how tolerant will she be of my mistakes, flaws, racist tendencies?" Try to focus more on the behavior and less on condemning the person.

When you are outraged, or even suggest that you're going to get involved by talking with the principal or the other person's parents, it can overwhelm and even further disempower your adopted teen. Justice and holding the offender accountable is important, but helping your teen to feel empowered is even more important. Try not to get ahead of them in how you respond.

Abby, Korean adoptee, 17, was residing in an all-white school system. She was a lesbian and often the recipient of derogatory comments pointing to her sexual orientation and to her race. One day as Abby left school to walk home, three boys on the football team made an offensive statement that included her sexual orientation and the "geisha girl" stereotype.

"I couldn't tell who said it," she said. "They were in a group and I'm pretty sure the coach heard it, too."

"Is there anything you can do that would help you to feel more empowered?" I asked.

"I don't know."

The following week, Abby told me, "I told the captain of the football team that my brother was looking for him." Then, she smiled. "He looked kind of scared."

Her brother had graduated two years earlier and had been a star hockey player at the school.

In that moment, Abby felt more empowered and confident. This was more valuable than justice.

Sometimes outrage can also take the form of political activism. I support and respect the conviction that many adoptive parents have against racism and other "isms." But is it possible to be too passionate? Yes. Your strong political stance can potentially make it harder for your teen to explore their racial identity.

Racism is a political cause, but it's also an area of your teen's identity, in a way that it wasn't when they were younger. But during these four to six years of teenhood, I'd recommend that you consider pulling back, which means being less angry, less vocal and less visible in advocating for racism and justice.

There's such a fine line between advocating for racial justice and equality and taking it from them. It's not uncommon for me to see adoptive parents who are very politically active with teens who have gone in the opposite direction.

Why?

Maybe they don't want you to be disappointed that they're not as fired up or as good at it, so they just don't even go there. Or maybe they just sense that the topic is unavailable. At times, with some adopted teens whose parents are politically active, I'll inquire about race issues and they'll say, "That's my parents' thing. You can ask them about that."

Let them be the expert, the leader.

When your teen downplays racism

There may be times when your teen may describe something as benign which you view as offensive and racist.

Eve, Chinese adoptee, 13, was showing her mom, Terry, her yearbook, which everyone in her grade had signed. But as Terry glanced through it something caught her attention. On the upper right-hand side, it said, "Miss you this summer! Now take your cute Asian self to get some sushi!" signed by a kid named David.

Terry was angry. What a rude, inappropriate racist thing to say, she thought. She approached Eve about it.

"Who is this person? David?" Terry asked, her brows furrowed.

"What? Nobody. He's a kid in my class."

"Didn't you read what he wrote?"

"Of course I did, Mom. What's the big deal?"

"What's the big deal? Well, it was offensive and racist! I'm very concerned that students are saying things like this in your school at all. Has this happened before?"

"Oh my god, Mom. He was just kidding! I knew you would make a big deal out of this! You always overreact about everything."

As you can see, Terry wasn't successful in bringing Abby to her side. She only succeeded in further polarizing the conversation. But that was a misplaced goal and doomed to fail anyway. The goal is to plant a seed.

What would that look like?

Something like this:

"I just read what David wrote. He's your classmate?"

"Yeah, why?"

"Did you think that what he wrote was racist or offensive?"

"Not really. I think he was just kidding around. Why, did you?"

"Well, yes I did. But he's your friend and you know him so you would probably have a better sense of that."

"Well, yeah, well he's not really my friend. Sometimes he can be a jerk, so...once he told this other Asian kid to be his grasshopper."

"How inappropriate!"

"I know! I thought the same thing!"

FINDING THE INSPIRATION

I remember, when I was an intern, sitting in a talk about race at work. There were 50–60 of us in the meeting.

One of other staff members said, "I have to say, when I heard about this talk today, I thought to myself, another racism talk, really? It gets so tiring to deal with it, when do I speak out, when do I not speak out? What do I say? And all of that."

I said, "If you're too tired to do it for yourself, then do it for me. Because I don't have a choice like you do."

As a white adoptive parent, it's in your hands how much you learn, how much you allow yourself to be vulnerable as you explore this issue of race and culture.

Just do as much as you possibly can, whatever that is for you.

Not for me but for you and your family.

Chapter 8

Mental Health and Survival for Adopted Teens

MENTAL HEALTH

Mental health issues are a risk factor for suicidality. Specifically, research states that 30 to 70 percent of those who completed a suicide suffered from major depression or bipolar disorder.

The National Institute of Mental Health (NIMH) defines major depression as a "common but serious mood disorder. It causes severe symptoms that affect how you feel, think, and handle daily activities, such as sleeping, eating, or working. To be diagnosed with depression, the symptoms must be present for at least two weeks."[1]

The NIMH states that bipolar disorder, "also known as manic-depressive illness, is a brain disorder that causes unusual shifts in mood, energy, activity levels, and the ability to carry out day-to-day tasks."[2]

---

1   Accessed on 06/01/17 at www.nimh.nih.gov/health/topics/depression/index.shtml

2   Accessed on 06/01/17 at www.nimh.nih.gov/health/topics/bipolar-disorder/index.shtml

Many years ago I attended a workshop by a young adopted Asian woman who spoke about her experience of being depressed and intermittently suicidal for most of her life. She felt incredibly guilty about it and confused as to why she continued to feel so badly about life and herself despite having a loving family. She decided to initiate a search for her birth mother and although she didn't meet her, she discovered that her mother had been institutionalized for depression and eventually committed suicide. Now, one might think that knowing this about her birth mother would cause her to feel even more disillusioned and perhaps maybe even more suicidal, knowing her genetic predisposition.

I asked, "How did it affect you to find that out about your birth mother?"

She answered, "I felt less alone. It was a relief. I thought, oh, that's why I'm like this."

I said, "So, it was better to know the truth, painful as it was."

She nodded, yes.

Being depressed was difficult, but not knowing or understanding the origins of her depression might have been even more difficult. Major depression is believed to be 40 to 50 percent heritability based on twin studies, which suggests that it is in part genetic and in part related to other factors such as environment.[3] Even if someone is genetically predisposed, it doesn't mean that they will be depressed. Research also suggested that adoptees are more likely to be depressed when one biological parent is also depressed.[4]

---

3   Levinson, Douglas F. (2006) "The genetics of depression: a review." *Biological Psychiatry 60*, 2, 84–92.

4   Tully, Erin C., Iacono, William G., and McGue, Matt (2008) "An adoption study of parental depression as an environmental liability for adolescent depression and childhood disruptive disorders." *The American Journal of Psychiatry 165*, 9, 1148–1154.

Background

Suicidality was less prevalent when I was growing up. Although safety was certainly on our minds, many of us worried more about being hurt by others than we did about hurting ourselves. But all of a sudden in my first year of college, it seemed all around me. An extended relative committed suicide, another made a serious attempt and several students in my peer group were psychiatrically hospitalized—some for suicide attempts, others for "self-harm" such as cutting themselves, still others for deep depression. It felt like an epidemic in my community, in my life. I was scared, angry and confused. My experience of being steeped in mental health issues—specifically, the life and death issue, suicidality, everywhere I turned—motivated me to better understand its complexity.

A few years ago, in my town, three high school students committed suicide in one school year. I've been told that one of them had an extensive history of mental health issues, another did not, and the third is not known. Our question, "Was this preventable?" is painful but important. And, as I've become increasingly immersed in the adoption community, I've asked myself that question in relation to adoptees. What do we need to know as a community about mental health and suicidality specifically pertaining to adopted teens and young adults?

I often work with adopted teens and young adults who struggle with finding value and meaning in their life. When they're struggling, they often question and doubt everything and everyone.

Another survival issue

Earlier in this book, I described the adoption story for some as one of survival. Adoptees survived a tenuous situation that others did not. Adoptees will often go to great lengths not to be abandoned again. Originally, they feared not being taken care of and getting their basic needs met. As children, that fear was mostly directed at their adoptive parents and caretakers. Mostly, they held adults responsible for how their life unfolded. Coming to terms with this experience was focused on accepting the *lack* of control that they had in how their lives unfolded.

"It wasn't your fault," people would say. "There was nothing that you could have done." They were dependent on the kindness of strangers. And, for the most part, their life was out of their hands.

But now things are a little bit different. Adopted teens are nearing adulthood. And, although their parents continue to hold a prominent role in their life, adopted teens recognize that they have a lot more power and control now.

Now, their life *is* in their hands.

Adopted teens go from too little to too much control, both of which can be terrifying. Part of growing up is learning that you have more power over yourself and your own life than anyone else. This awareness can feel overwhelming for many adopted teens and, for some, unbearable. Suicidality is also centered on survival. I would argue that for some adopted teens, suicidality becomes part of their continuing story as a survivor.

Research tells us that adopted teens are four times more likely to make a suicide attempt.[5] In order to better understand

---

5   Keyes, Margaret A., Malone, Stephen M., Sharma, Anu, Iacono, William G. and McGue, Matthew (2013) "Risk of suicide attempt in adopted and nonadopted offspring." *Pediatrics 132*, 4, 639–646.

what they're going through, it's not enough to ask, "Are you feeling suicidal?" Their relationship to suicidality cannot be distilled down to a "yes" or a "no" answer.

There are certain themes that may shed some light on why adopted teens are at higher risk. Those themes are survival, mental health, anger and identity. We'll delve into those, then talk about being proactive and getting the help that you need.

As an adoptive parent, you're faced with the daunting task of being informed but not consumed by the life and death stakes of this topic. Perhaps a part of you is summoning that old saying, "If it ain't broke, why fix it? They're fine!" Some fear that putting suicide on the table, even in unspoken ways, may encourage it somehow. I understand that concern but that hasn't been my experience. Eight out of ten people considering suicide give some sign of their intentions. Raising your awareness is less risky in the long run.

A "survival" story

This case example does not represent the feelings and experiences of adopted teens. My hope is to deepen your understanding of the ways of just how the survival theme can surface.

Tanya, 15, Chinese adoptee, had been hospitalized several months earlier because of suicidal ideation—suicidal thoughts without a specific plan.

"She's really depressed. She just isolates herself at school. She told me that she thinks that she's ugly, that no guy would ever want to date her," her mom Amy said in the initial parent meeting. "I keep trying to tell her how beautiful she is but she just says that the other girls are prettier. I ask her why she would feel that way but she can't really explain it."

"The other girls in her grade are white?" I asked.

Amy nodded, yes.

"After she was hospitalized last October, she started seeing a therapist but in recent weeks has been saying that she doesn't want to keep going. I don't know. It didn't seem to be going anywhere. Plus, I felt like Tanya needs someone who is also Asian and adopted. It's just mother's intuition but I feel like that's where a lot of this is coming from."

This is a conversation that Tanya and I had after she had been coming in for about a month. Tanya sat on my couch, her shoulders rounded, her long straight dark hair was barely brushed away from her eyes.

"It's just like, I just sometimes wish I wasn't here anymore," she said, quiet but not tearful.

"Do you think that you deserve to be here?" I asked calmly.

Tanya thought for a second, her gaze just below eye contact. She shrugged.

"I don't know," she said, as she turned her cell phone on and off in her hand.

"That's interesting, right? That you're not sure about that?"

"I was a mistake. My birth mom gave me up," she said, and looked right at me. I glimpsed the flash of anger in her eyes which I hadn't seen before.

"As in, your birth mom didn't want you? That kind of mistake?"

"Yeah, pretty much."

"You're angry about that, aren't you?" I wanted to acknowledge what we both already knew.

Tanya didn't answer.

Then she said, "Why didn't she just have an abortion?"

"Would you have preferred that?"

"Sometimes."

"You think about that, don't you? That if she had just made a different decision, you wouldn't be here. And, in your darkest days, you probably wish that she *had* made a different decision. Life has been hard, painful."

Tanya didn't say anything but her eyes were full of anger now. It was directed at me but I knew that it went deeper.

I said, "I know that you've been depressed for a long time, but I think you've also been really angry. That part of you, those feelings, are really important for us to learn more about."

For some adopted teens the fear of survival can be as strong as the fear of death. The fact that there was a decision, one that could have changed everything, can be haunting.

NARRATIVE OF THE TRAGIC HERO

Along with life and death, there is another theme in my work which includes suicidality that I've seen a lot. This theme is what I describe as the "tragic hero" narrative. The "tragic hero" had its origins in Greek mythology, defined as "a great or virtuous character in a dramatic tragedy who is destined for downfall, suffering, or defeat."[6] The tragic hero suffers more than they deserve and is physically and/or spiritually wounded by their experiences, which often result in death. The tragic hero is a sympathetic character, someone whom their audience wants to see happy. But their world inevitably falls to pieces, despite their best intentions, and comes to a tragic end. They are ultimately doomed to fail: fated to just miss everything they could ever want and need.

Spencer, 19, adopted from Guatemala, had been coming in to see me for almost a year. He thought about suicide a lot,

---

6   Dictionary.com (2017) 'Tragic Hero.' Accessed on 01/02/17 at www.dictionary.com/browse/tragic-hero

but had never made an attempt. He talked about his life in dramatic broad strokes, almost as if he was starring in his own play. Everyone who spent time with him loved him, particularly adults. His parents bent over backwards trying to make his life work, but nothing they did seemed to help. Spencer's emotional pain about his life, his birth mother and his depression was real. He hated how depressed he was and how much he continually disappointed those who were so dedicated and loving. But he also spun countless fantasies, about being rich, about being in the perfect relationship. Yes, to some degree, that's what many young adults do; but for Spencer, it went deep. He had the makings of a tragic hero. When life begins in the context of tragedy, ending in tragedy can feel fated. There's the illusion of continuity and cohesion in the life of a tragic hero, which seemed previously out of reach.

But if he were to commit suicide he would no longer be his own audience member. He would not be able to witness the tragic end that he had so painstakingly constructed. What did Spencer imagine they might say? "Oh, Spencer was so young. This just breaks my heart. He had so much potential. He was so loved. He was ripped away from us too soon. What a tragedy."

To begin tragically can lend itself to a tragic end, but the future hasn't been written yet. Just because Spencer's life began in tragedy doesn't mean that it has to end in one. I needed him to become more aware of what he was playing out, as the first step in overriding it.

REMORSE

I met Nina when she entered a crisis stabilization unit for adolescents, a safe, secure place where adolescents reside for a few days. She had contemplated suicide off and on for the past few months but hadn't made an attempt. She and her dad were close and she often talked with him about her feelings of self-loathing and shame. Her grades had slipped, she was disillusioned with her friends and just going through the motions with her boyfriend who was often rude and offensive towards her. Some of the other boys in school were even worse.

Referring to the guys at school she said, "I just think, like, 'If that's what they want, they really hate having me around so much, then I should just not be here.'"

"You think that if you killed yourself, that would be a wake-up call for these guys?"

"Yeah, then they would realize what they've been doing to me all of this time. Maybe they'd see how hard it is."

I was aware of Nina's anger, but also of the power of her fantasy.

I said, "So, they would realize what they did to you and feel terrible. 'How could we have done that to her!'"

Nina nodded, her eyes narrowing, face stony, her anger beginning to surface.

"Listen, Nina, I can see how you could come to imagine that. I can see how there would be a sense of satisfaction and power in doing to them what they've done to you. But I don't think it would be the wake-up call that you're hoping for. They might feel bad for a few minutes, or a few hours, maybe a day or two, but then they'll go on with their lives and, in the end, you'll have sacrificed your life. They haven't earned that kind of power over you. They just haven't.

You have a future, a future that doesn't include them. Don't let them take that away from you."

SUICIDALITY AND THE "GOOD ADOPTEE"

There are certain adopted teens who look like they have it all together. They make it look easy. They have lots of friends, are loved by their dedicated family, enjoy sports, are doing well in school—just have tons of future potential. And, although they may have certain life challenges medically, or perhaps academically, they seem like they're admirably rising to the occasion.

When it comes to their feelings about being adopted and/or relinquished, they seem well adjusted and accepting, that they feel lucky to have had the opportunities that they had.

This is the "good" adoptee. But it's not the whole story. The part that doesn't show is the struggle, the turmoil, the doubt and the anger. The good adoptee has adapted almost *too* well, and is *too* attuned to the needs and longings of others. They are *too* virtuous and self-sacrificing.

Perhaps you're wondering, "How can you be too much of those things? Isn't that what we want as parents, to raise good people?"

Yes, when it's authentic. But the good adoptee may have conflicting agendas that they've successfully hidden from even themselves. They want to ensure that they won't be abandoned or rejected. They do this by making sure that they are indispensable, someone that no one can afford to lose.

And, when some choose to take their own life, it seems like it comes out of nowhere.

Potential red flags with "good" adoptees:

- Do adults who meet them just love them, sometimes even more than their peers?

- Do they avoid conflict?

- Do they ever talk with you about imperfect feelings like disappointment, anger, etc.?

- Do they ever hurt your feelings or do they always know just what to say?

- Are they very sensitive and soak up the feelings of others?

The good adoptee may already be able to intuitively sense what you're feeling or even believe that they know what's best for you. And, if and when the good adoptee gets into emotional trouble, their thinking can become distorted. In that compromised, hidden state, they may decide that what's best for everyone is for them to take matters into their own hands. They believe that you're better off without them.

LISTENING, LEARNING AND RESPONDING

Our path

The American Foundation for Suicide Prevention states that, although there is no one cause, "Suicide most often occurs when stressors exceed current coping abilities of someone suffering from a mental health condition."[7]

The purpose of taking this path with your adopted teen—unrescuing, setting limits, connecting conversations and envisioning the future—is that it is a way for you to proactively address your teen's needs, support your relationship and pave their way into adulthood. Don't underestimate the power of that. That said, suicidality is powerful, too.

---

7   Accessed on 06/01/17 at https://afsp.org/about-suicide/risk-factors-and-warning-signs

The AASF tells us that suicide warning signs *may* include:

- if the teen talks about feeling trapped, being a burden, or having no reason to live

- sudden changes in behavior or mood shifts, particularly after a stressful event

- depression and bipolar disorder

- being bullied or other life stressors such as death, including other suicides.

Getting the help that you need

No one can ever guarantee the safety of your adopted teen—whether parent, therapist, or teacher. But most agree that leaving issues unaddressed leaves you more vulnerable, more at risk. It's so important to do what you can to get the help that you need even if that means making it work financially and/or logistically. Nowadays there are so many options of therapists, schools of thought, styles, etc. There are also a whole host of modalities—individual, family, parent guidance, group and so forth. There are also different ways to intervene besides therapy like a structured time-limited program, medication, neurofeedback, drug rehab, to name a few. Then there are different levels of care beyond therapy such as day treatment programs, residential, inpatient and wilderness.

It's crazy. And, yet, I would argue that your first task is to find your adopted teen a therapist. It doesn't have to be an adoption therapist, although that can be beneficial. But let me put it this way. I would take a nonadopted therapist I felt more comfortable with over an adoption therapist I felt less comfortable with. I would argue that, even beyond how much they know about adoption, or what their therapeutic modality is, I focus on two broad, intuition-based questions:

- Can I potentially learn from this person (for my daughter or son)?

- Can I learn to trust this person over time?

Note that I didn't include whether or not you like the person. You can learn a lot from someone who is different from you, or whom you wouldn't want to go to tea with if you had the option. That's okay. That's not as important. I had one client, an adopted teen, Stacy, whom I saw from fourth grade through high school and beyond. She told her mom that she wasn't too fond of me, but that I was like Ms. Johnson, her third grade teacher. Ms. Johnson was her least favorite teacher but she learned the most from her. She almost prided herself on it after a while. She would start sessions by saying, "You know that we don't get along, right?"

Should they start therapy? If so, when?

Some research[8] has suggested that adoptive parents are quicker to put their children in therapy, which may factor into the higher numbers of adopted children and teens in therapy compared to those not adopted. When there's a clear concerning precipitant such as excessive crying, or feelings of hopelessness, you should absolutely initiate therapy.

On the other hand, you don't want to dilute the potency of therapy by bringing them in before it's time. If there's no precipitant but you just feel like they could use someone to talk to, I would consider holding off. If you're not sure whether or not to be concerned, you could consult a therapist who sees teens and get their take on the situation.

---

8   Warren, S.B. (1992) "Lower threshold for referral for psychiatric treatment for adopted adolescents." *Journal of the American Academy of Child and Adolescent Psychiatry 31*, 3, 512–517.

How do you introduce the idea of therapy?

Let's say that you've decided that it's definitely a good time to get started. Here's one way to have this conversation:

> *"Hey Joe, listen, I wanted to touch base with you about something. You know, it's not uncommon for people to get additional help for stuff that's been difficult. You've seemed so down since school started and I thought it would be a good time to start seeing someone, a therapist."*

> Joe: *"No way. I'm not seeing a therapist, not going to happen. I'm fine."*

> *"Well, maybe so, but still, I think it would be good to add some supports. I want you to feel comfortable with who you have, so if you want, we can see two or three once and that way I can get your perspective on who might make the most sense. There's a woman in Newton who also happens to be adopted and I thought that she might be an option."*

> *"Newton's too far away. I'm not taking the train there from school. That's a pain."*

> *"Okay, well, I can drive you the first time and we can go from there."*

> *"Fine."*

There were three tips from this conversation that I want to highlight.

1. Don't try to convince them how troubled they are; they're just likely trying to save face by saying that they're fine.

2. Let them have input on who it is.

3. They're just committing to the first session, not to launch a therapeutic relationship. That's too much of a leap.

REMEMBER...

This is no reason to panic. Being informed and proactive is incredibly important. Managing your fears is one of the hardest parts. And following this path— unrescuing, limits, conversations and the future—is your best chance of emotional safety.

Chapter 9

Put Your Oxygen Mask on First

On planes, the flight attendant says, "If you are travelling with a young child or a person who needs assistance, put your own oxygen mask on first before assisting others."

Heather, adoptive parent of three, had her hands full. Alexa, adopted from Ethiopia, was 15, Jess was adopted from China and was 13 and Sarah, adopted from Korea, was nine. Alexa was in residential treatment, stayed there during the week and had home visits on weekends. Things had been worsening. It was after a particularly difficult weekend that she got in touch with me.

"It was all going along swimmingly," Heather said in her parent meeting.

"We had bread in the oven, the fire was going in the fireplace and we all played cards. Everything was just perfect! Then, Alexa's friend called and asked her to go for a movie that night. We get into this thing about the curfew and, before you know it, they're all going at it. Alexa's yelling and screaming, 'I hate you!' Then she pushes a stack of books off the kitchen table all over the floor. Sarah starts crying and goes to her room. Jess, still with her apron on, was like, 'Not again! This happens every weekend!' And I burned the bread! Can you believe it?"

Heather sighed. "It seems like this happens every weekend. It starts out fine and then something happens and it just deteriorates. I'm so worn down. I don't know. I can't even see straight sometimes. I know I should be more patient."

Heather shook her head. Then she gestured under her eyelids at the dark circles.

"Look at me! I'm a wreck! I don't know what else to do."

"You guys have been through so much. It's no wonder that you're debilitated. That's too much for any family."

Heather nodded.

"A few things. It sounds like you're so good at cultivating a warm, family-like atmosphere with the bread baking and everything, but given how compromised your girls' history of abuse and neglect has been, I wonder whether it might feel too pressured for them. In their mind, they're so far from the Norman Rockwell family and if they sense that that's what you want, it can raise a lot of feelings for them, like guilt and worrying about disappointing you. I'm wondering whether it might make sense to tone it down a bit. It's enjoyable to spend time as a family, but it doesn't have be as special."

Heather nodded, agreeingly. "Okay, I see what you're saying. So, not the bread?"

"Right, or just any project or activity that has to go smoothly the whole way through in order to turn out well. But I'm also thinking about just how exhausting it is to parent your children right now. Do you and your husband, you know, ever go out, spend time together without the kids?"

Heather blinked. "Go out? Like for dinner? Oh, we haven't been out in months. I can't remember the last time that we did something like that. It's hard to find a sitter for the kids, they're so difficult…"

"Right! Even more reason to make it happen," I said and smiled.

Heather thought for a second, "We have talked about how we've wanted to go away for like an overnight or weekend, or something. There's been so much going on. We just forgot about it."

"Do you happen to know anyone who might be able to stay with the kids if you were to plan something like that?"

"Well, actually my mother is just about 25 minutes away. She might be willing to stay with them. They love her."

Heather did go away with her husband for the weekend. She talked about it at our next meeting.

"It was great for us to get away. We relaxed and I actually was able to do some reading! I did end up reading some adoption and parenting books and finished a novel that I'd put on the back burner. And, when we got back, I was just so happy to see the kids."

Then Heather said, "They all came and hugged me. But the thing is, I had no expectations."

It wasn't that Heather literally had *no* expectations. But she was able to really see them in ways that she hadn't before. Heather put a value on her wellbeing, allowing her to be more open, generous and loving with her family.

Why is it important to include self-care on your priority list? You'll live longer. And that's important. But you're also a role model. You value yourself and your life and your family. You feel empowered, and if not, you find ways to address that. You don't make decisions based on fear and trepidation, and expect the same from your teen.

However, it's also important to strive to accept wherever and whoever you are in this moment, warts and all! No need to be critical or judgmental even when you fall short, which you inevitably will. Feeling vulnerable is part of any parent's journey who wants to stretch beyond their comfort zone into their growth zone. And, if and when you feel at a loss, hopeless, just begin again, wherever you left off. That's a great place to start.

Resources

ORGANIZATIONS/WEBSITES

A Home Within

www.ahomewithin.org

A national organization that provides open-ended individual therapy to current and former foster care youth, free of charge. Also trains those working with traumatized and/or troubled youth in relationship-based practices for trauma-informed care.

Adoption Community of New England

www.rfkchildren.org/acone

ACONE educates, supports and advocates on behalf of all members of the adoption triad: birth parents, adoptive parents and adoptees. It assists members through all stages of their adoption-related experiences.

Adoptive Families

www.adoptivefamilies.com

This provides a wealth of information regarding adopting and adoption through a digital magazine along with online support forums and resources.

Adoptive Families Together (AFT)

AFT is a supportive membership network of adoptive parents who share combined experiences and information to strengthen their families and adoptions. It is part of Massachusetts Society for the Prevention of Cruelty to Children.

Adoption Today and *Fostering Families Today* magazines

www.adoptinfo.net

Adoption Today offers guidance around international and domestic adoption. *Fostering Families Today* explores issues that affect families and children.

American Foundation for Suicide Prevention (AFSP)

www.asfp.org

The AFSP raises awareness, funds scientific research and provides resources and aid to those affected by suicide.

Catalyst Foundation

www.catalystfoundation.org/camp-tour

Supports community programs to provide basic needs to prevent the trafficking of young children. Also offers family weekend camps and cultural tours.

Center on the Developing Child, Harvard University

www.developingchild.harvard.edu

The mission of the Center on the Developing Child is to drive science-based innovation that achieves breakthrough outcomes for children facing adversity.

Children and Adults with Attention Deficit Disorder (CHADD)

www.chadd.org

An organization which provides education, advocacy and support for individuals with ADHD. CHADD also publishes a variety of online and printed materials to keep members current on research advances, medications and treatments affecting individuals with ADHD.

Child Trauma Academy (CTA)

www.childtrauma.org

The CTA is a not-for-profit organization based in Houston, Texas working to improve the lives of high-risk children through direct service, research and education.

Child Information Gateway

www.childwelfare.gov

Child Welfare Information Gateway offers information and tools on topics such as child welfare, child abuse and neglect and adoption.

Coram BAAF Adoption and Fostering Academy

http://corambaaf.org.uk

This focuses on supporting and developing all areas of permanency in the UK – adoption, fostering and kinship care as well as returning children to their parents.

Depression & Bipolar Support Alliance

www.dbsalliance.org

The DBSA provides hope, help, support and education to improve the lives of people who have mood disorders.

Families with Children from China

www.fwcc.org

FCC is a nondenominational organization of families who have adopted children from China. It is a network of support for families who've adopted in China and provides information to prospective parents.

Federation for Children with Special Needs

http://fcsn.org

Provides information, support and assistance to parents of children with disabilities, their professional partners and communities.

Friends of Russian and Ukranian Adoption and Neighbouring Countries (FRUA)

www.frua.org

FRUA offers families hope, help and community by providing connection, education, resources and advocacy, and works to improve the lives of orphaned children.

Jewish Children and Family Services

www.jfcsboston.org

This provides adoption resources for the community, including groups, workshops and ongoing support.

Kazakh Aul of the United States

www.kazakh-aul-us.org

Together with their families, children participate in Kazakh heritage camps and cultural education to develop a deeper sense of knowledge and understanding of their birth culture, and how they fit into both the Kazakh and American worlds.

Korean-American Adoptee Network (KAAN)

kaanet.org

The Korean American Adoptee Network offers an annual conferences and resources for the Korean-adoptee families through the life cycle. It is unique in that it is inclusive of all ages and constellations of family.

National Child Traumatic Stress Network (NCTSN)

www.nctsn.org

The NCTSN's collaboration of frontline providers, researchers and families is committed to raising the standard of care while increasing access to services. Combining knowledge of child development, expertise in the full range of child traumatic experiences and dedication to evidence-based practices, the NCTSN changes the course of children's lives by changing the course of their care.

National Council on Adoptable Children (NACAC)

www.nacac.org

This organization has legal, ethical and practice influences on children's adoption issues. It is a powerful advocacy organization and leads in improving adoption practices.

National Foster Care and Adoption Directory

www.childwelfare.gov/nfcad/

This section of the federal Children's Bureau, Administration for Children and Families, US Department of Health and Human Services Child Welfare Information Gateway provides information about all aspects of adoption and foster care.

Society of Special Needs Adoptive Parents (SNAP)

www.specialneedsabilityprogram.org

SNAP provides opportunities to the special needs communities that are not always funded through local, state and federal programs.

BOOKS

Dweck, Carol (2012) *Mindset: Changing the Way You Think to Fulfil Your Potential.* New York: Ballantine Books.

If you are a parent, a teacher, a coach or a person who struggles with feeling like life is a series of obstacles, read this book and learn how it is always possible to change and live a more fulfilled life.

Kent, Rose (2010) *Kimchi & Calamari.* New York: HarperCollins.

About a 14-year-old boy, Joseph Calderaro, who is adopted from Korea but is raised Italian. He is assigned an essay on his ancestors. It's hard for him to decide which heritage to write about.

Oh, Arissa H. (2015) *To Save the Children of Korea: The Cold War Origins of International Adoption.* Stanford, CA: Stanford University Press.

The first book about the origins and history of international adoption.

Pertman, Adam (2011) *Adoption Nation.* Boston, MA: The Harvard Common Press.

Explores the history and human impact of adoption, explodes the corrosive myths surrounding it, and tells compelling stories about its participants as they grapple with issues relating to race, identity, equality, discrimination, personal history and connections with all their families.

Willing, Indigo, Kolbe, Anh Đào, Golding, Dominic, Holtan, Tim *et al.* (2015) *Vietnamese Adopted: A Collection of Voices.* CQT Media and Publishing.

This is a group of writings each in their own form and style. Shaped by their own experiences, observations, country and language, it is the goal of this book to make these narratives, opinions and perspectives available to the greater adopted and Vietnamese communities.

Christian, Diane René and Transue-Woolston, Amanda H.L. (eds) (2013) *Perpetual Child: Dismantling the Stereotype.* The An-Ya Project.

A collection of stories, poems, and essays aimed at confronting the "perpetual child" stereotype faced by adult adoptees.

Solomon, Andrew (2013) *Far From the Tree: Parents, Children and the Search for Identity.* London: Chatto and Windus.

Andrew Solomon tells the stories of parents who not only learn to deal with their exceptional children but also find profound meaning in doing so. Solomon mines the eloquence of ordinary people facing extreme challenges.

Harris O'Connor, Susan (2012) *The Harris Narratives: An Introspective Study of a Transracial Adoptee.* Arlington, MA: The Pumping Station.

This book consists of five autobiographical narratives by Susan Harris O'Connor, a social worker and transracial adoptee.

Jacobs, Debra, Chin Ponte, Iris and Wang, Leslie Kim (2010) *From Home to Homeland: What Adoptive Families Need to Know before Making a Return Trip to China.* Yeong & Yeong Book Company.

Authors explore the joys and challenges of traveling to China.

Christian, Diane René, Rosita Gozález and Transue
Woolston, Amanda H.L. (2015) *Flip the Script: Adult
Adoptee Anthology.* The An-Ya Project.
This anthology offers readers a diverse compilation of literature and artistry
from a global community of adoptees.

Pavao, Joyce (2005) *The Family of Adoption.* Boston,
MA: Beacon Press.
Full of wonderful stories that give insight into a wide variety of adoption
issues, describes the developmental stages and challenges one can expect in
the life of the adopted person.

O'Malley, Beth (2000) *Lifebooks: Creating a Treasure
for the Adopted Child.* Winthrop, MA: Adoption-Works.
Adoptionlifebooks.com
Step-by-step guidance on how to create a lifebook along with valuable insights
from her experiences as an adoptee and social worker. Helpful newsletter, too.

TRANSMEDIA PROJECT

Touching Home in China: In Search of Missing Girlhoods
Transmedia project written and produced by Melissa Ludtke. These US teens
hang out with "hometown" Chinese girls who teach them about what it's like
growing up as a girl in twent-first century China.

MOVIES

Somewhere Between directed by Linda Goldstein
Knowlton
This documentary film follows the lives of four teenaged girls adopted from
China and now living in the United States.

First Person Plural directed by Deann Borshay Liem

This is an intensely personal and moving film that chronicles Borshay's efforts to reconcile her life as the adopted daughter of a loving American family with her previously unknown life in Korea.

Off and Running directed by Nicole Opper

When Avery's curiosity about her African-American roots grows, she decides to contact her birth mother. This choice propels Avery into her own complicated exploration of race, identity, and family that threatens to distance her from the parents she's always known.

PODCASTS

The Rambler, by Mike McDonald, Korean-adoptee

This is an hour-long, one-on-one interview podcast centered around international and transracial adoption and the people involved.

Adoptees On, by Haley Radke, Canadian adoptee

Stories from adoptees that often include the complex experience of searching for birth parents and for some, reunion.